Around the WORLD in 80 WORDS

Around the WORLD in 80 WORDS

A Journey through the English Language

PAUL ANTHONY JONES

THE
UNIVERSITY
OF CHICAGO
PRESS

The University of Chicago Press, Chicago 60637
© 2018 by Paul Anthony Jones
All rights reserved. No part of this book may be used or reproduced in
any manner whatsoever without written permission, except in the case
of brief quotations in critical articles and reviews. For more information,
contact the University of Chicago Press, 1427 E. 60th St., Chicago, IL
60637.
Published 2020
Printed in the United States of America

29 28 27 26 25 24 23 22 21 20   1 2 3 4 5

ISBN-13: 978-0-226-68279-2 (paper)
ISBN-13: 978-0-226-68282-2 (e-book)
DOI: https://doi.org/10.7208/chicago/9780226682822.001.0001

First published in Great Britain by Elliott and Thompson Limited, 2018.

Library of Congress Cataloging-in-Publication Data

Names: Jones, Paul Anthony, 1983– author.
Title: Around the world in 80 words : a journey through the English
    language / Paul Anthony Jones.
Description: Chicago : University of Chicago Press, 2020. | Includes
    bibliographical references.
Identifiers: LCCN 2019037139 | ISBN 9780226682792 (paperback) |
    ISBN 9780226682822 (ebook)
Subjects: LCSH: English language—Etymology. | Names, Geographical.
Classification: LCC PE1578.A2 J66 2020 | DDC 422—dc23
LC record available at https://lccn.loc.gov/2019037139

♾ This paper meets the requirements of ANSI/NISO Z39.48-1992
(Permanence of Paper).

For my parents,
Leon and Maureen

A book that travels, for everyone who can't

CONTENTS

CONTENTS

INTRODUCTION

I t's easy to forget that place names – just like first names, surnames, the days of the week and months of the year – are all still just words at the end of the day. As such, they have meanings, histories and etymologies all their own.

London, for instance, is thought to be the descendant of an ancient Celtic word perhaps meaning something along the lines of 'town at the unfordable part of the river'.* *Britain*, meanwhile,

---

* Actually, the name *London* is something of an etymological mystery, and this theory – proposed in 1998 by Professor Richard Coates, then President of the English Place-Name Society – is just one of a number of possible explanations.

If not a Celtic word referring to the relative uncrossability of the Thames, *London* might be a Welsh-origin name meaning something like 'lake fortress'. Or else it could derive from the name of the Roman goddess of the moon, Luna.

Or perhaps, as another theory claims, it takes its name from an old Celtic warrior, whose supposed name, *Londino*, might have meant something like 'fierce' or 'wild'? Or maybe, as the twelfth-century historian Geoffrey of Monmouth claimed, the name derives from Lud Silver-Hand – a king from Welsh folklore, who is said to have saved Wales both from a plague of dragons, and from a magical giant who had the power

probably derives from an equally ancient Celtic word, meaning 'tattooed people' – a somewhat appropriate name for what is now believed to be the most tattooed nation in Europe.

And it doesn't stop there. *Casablanca* literally means 'white house'. *Beijing* means 'northern capital', *Nanjing* means 'southern capital', and *Tokyo* means 'eastern capital'. *Chicago* means 'place of the wild onion'. *Topeka* means 'good place to dig potatoes'. And *Cleveland*, Ohio, was named after its founder, Moses Cleaveland; according to local folklore, the extra A in Cleaveland's name was dropped so that it could fit more easily on the front page of the local newspaper.

The Sudanese capital, *Khartoum*, has a name meaning 'end of the elephant's trunk'. The Tajikistani capital, *Dushanbe*, literally means 'Monday'* – a reference to the fact that the city grew from a regular weekly market held on that day. And *Funafuti*, the capital city of the tiny Pacific nation of Tuvalu, has a name that means 'banana woman'.†

But what if we were to turn these etymologies around? So instead of looking at the origins of the place names in our atlases and gazetteers, we look at the origins of the words in the dictionary that are themselves derived from place names? By doing that, we suddenly have a whole new set of stories to tell.

Some words of this kind – let's call them 'geonyms' – seem obvious when you think about it. *Turkeys*, *Brazil nuts* and *Panama*

---

to send people to sleep by playing music; to escape the giant's soporific tunes, Geoffrey explained, Lud dipped his head in a bucket of water. (On second thoughts, that last theory isn't quite as reliable as the others . . .)

* Actually, it *literally* means 'two days after Saturday'.

† *Funa* is a feminine-forming suffix in the native Tuvaluan language, while *futi* literally means 'banana'. The name *Funafuti* – 'banana woman' – is said to have originally belonged to one of the two wives of Telematua, the ancestral founder of the Tuvaluan nation, who supposedly named the town in her honour.

hats are all familiar examples, as are *French fries*, *Danish pastries* and *Jerusalem artichokes*. But the stories behind even these familiar terms aren't quite as straightforward as you might presume.

Turkeys don't actually come from Turkey, after all, and nor do Jerusalem artichokes come from Israel. So what happened there? And as soon as you start to find out that Panama hats come from Ecuador not Panama, and that French fries were invented across the border in Belgium – well, things start to take something of an interesting detour . . .

It's etymological stories precisely like these that bring us here now – at the start of a grand tour both of the world, and of the English dictionary. Ahead of us lies a 70,000-mile route, as the crow flies, and an itinerary comprised entirely of towns and villages, cities and countries (and at least one mountain) whose names have, in some way or another, become immortalised in our language.

Our journey will begin in London, from where we'll head out across to France, Belgium, Germany and the Netherlands, then north into Scandinavia, east into Russia, and south to the Mediterranean. From the Balkans, Central Europe, Spain and Portugal, we'll travel down through Africa, north to the Middle East, then out across Central Asia to the Far East. From there, we'll turn south once more, down through the islands of the western Pacific Ocean and stopping off for etymological tours of Japan, the Philippines, Indonesia, Australia and New Zealand.

Jumping across the Pacific Ocean, we'll land in the far north of North America, making stops in Alaska, Canada, the western USA, and marking the 50,000-mile mark of our journey in Mexico. From there, destinations in Central and South America will take us as far south as the Falkland Islands, before we enter the home straight – heading north through the likes of Brazil, Bermuda, the eastern United States and Canada, before a solitary stop in Iceland breaks up our return journey across the Atlantic, back to the British Isles.

It will be an epic trip, no doubt about it. And along the way, there are some of the dictionary's most extraordinary etymological stories to tell.

The tiny town in rural France that almost brought down the German government lies ahead of us. As does a valley outside Düsseldorf that gave us a word that altered our perception of human history. We'll find out why a tiny Swedish mining town now finds itself honoured alongside the likes of Albert Einstein and Marie Curie, and what the people of fifty of the world's nations owe to a tiny spa town on the Czech–German border. The story of how a village in South Africa gave us a word for a tactical demotion makes our list, as does the Jordanian mountain whose name has become a byword for a tantalising glimpse. And we'll find out what the Philippines has given to your office in-tray, what Alaska has given to your liquor cabinet, and how a speech given by a bumbling North Carolinian gave us a word for impenetrable nonsense.

But every journey, as the old saying goes, starts with a single step. And ours starts with a step along a long-forgotten street in the south of London . . .

1

LONDON, UK

Kent Street ejectment

Bags packed? Passport ready? Good, because we'll be making no fewer than eighty stops on this etymological trip around the world. And following the route of another literary circumnavigation, we're beginning this journey in London.

But while Phileas Fogg's eighty-day voyage began in the lavish surroundings of the Reform Club, we're starting off in – well, a less grandiose setting. A poverty-stricken street in eighteenth-century Southwark, to be exact.

Places all across London have provided inspiration for countless words and phrases over the centuries, from an *Aldgate draught*, a punning name for a bad cheque (so called as Aldgate was once home to a well-used water pump) to a *Westminster wedding*, an eighteenth-century term for what one contemporary dictionary defined as 'a whore and a rogue married together'. An interesting take on the Abbey's popularity as a high-society wedding venue.

Because inmates at London's Newgate prison were typically coupled together in pairs, to walk *Newgate fashion* is to walk hand in hand, while a *Newgate nightingale* was once a witty nickname for a jailbird in seventeenth-century slang. If you've ever been in financial difficulty then you've been *on Carey Street*, the Holborn address of the Bankruptcy Department of London's Supreme

Court (which now lies, somewhat ironically, beside the London School of Economics).

And if you've ever just missed the Tube or found yourself stuck in an endless London traffic jam, then you may have had cause to use *Billingsgate*, a seventeenth-century word for coarse language namechecking the notoriously vulgar-tongued vendors of London's fish market.

On the opposite side of the River Thames from all these was Kent Street. You won't find its name on any maps of London today, but you will at least find it in the dictionary under the heading of a *Kent Street ejectment*.

Kent Street was one of London's most ancient thoroughfares, thought to have developed from a Roman road that once connected the city to Greenwich, Canterbury and Dover. Originally, little more than fields and open ground lay either side of it, but as London thrived this empty greenbelt was gradually eaten up by a sprawling network of houses and hostels, inns and taverns, and one of the city's largest leprosy hospitals.

As a main road in and out of the city, by 1565 Kent Street had grown in significance enough to warrant the passing of an Act of Parliament ordering that it be paved. This sparked a further boom in housebuilding and development, but unfortunately for Kent Street, these dwellings were far from the most luxurious homes in the capital, and their tenants were far from the most affluent.

Soon, the entire Kent Street area had become synonymous with the very worst of London's squalor and destitution, and those who ventured into it were quick to ensure they didn't repeat the journey. In his *Survey of London* (1720), the English historian John Strype described Kent Street as 'very long but ill-built', and 'chiefly inhabited by broom-men and mumpers' (or street-sweepers and beggars, as we'd know them today). In his *Travels Through France and Italy* (1766), the Scottish writer Tobias Smollett labelled Kent Street 'a most disgraceful entrance to such an opulent city', that gave anyone unfamiliar with the capital 'such an idea of misery and meanness . . . all the wealth and magnificence of London and Westminster are afterwards unable to destroy'.

Another equally evocative account from the late 1800s lamented Kent Street's 'evil reputation', and described a street where it was not uncommon to find 'men, women, children, asses, pigs, and dogs . . . living together in the same room'. Even Charles Dickens thought it 'the worst kept part of London' (second only to Haymarket, in his opinion), while one nineteenth-century dictionary spelled it out even more clearly: in a description of precisely what constitutes living the 'high' and 'low' life in London in the early 1800s, the lexicographer John Badcock had this to say:

> *White Cross Street, of a Saturday night, is low; and so is Petticoat Lane of a Sunday morning; and Kent Street, all day.*
> —John Badcock, *Slang: A Dictionary of the Turf* (1823)

All day every day, there was seemingly no escaping how 'low' life was on Kent Street. Its inhabitants were among the city's poorest, their homes among its most miserable, and their landlords among its least sympathetic.

No matter the meagre circumstances, there was still rent to be collected on Kent Street, and woe betide anyone who fell into arrears. With no property worth seizing to cover the debt, insolvent tenants on Kent Street would often find themselves being swiftly and unceremoniously evicted via an uncompromising method that became known as the *Kent Street ejectment*:

> *Kent Street ejectment. To take away the street door [of a house]: a method practised by the landlords in Kent Street, Southwark, when their tenants are above a fortnight's rent in arrear.*
> —Francis Grose, *A Classical Dictionary of the Vulgar Tongue* (1785)

That definition is the earliest record we have of a *Kent Street ejectment*, suggesting that the practice first emerged among the stoniest of the stony-hearted landlords of mid-eighteenth-century London. Use of the term (and, we can presume, the practice) steadily dwindled throughout the 1800s, and the expression has long since gathered dust in one of the more neglected corners of the dictionary; it's remained little more than a historical and linguistic curio since the turn of the twentieth century.

Kent Street itself, meanwhile, has long since changed: renamed Tabard Street in 1877, after redevelopment and renovation in the early 1900s it's now a perfectly respectable neighbourhood standing in the shadow of The Shard, one of modern London's most impressive landmarks, and no longer one of the city's main arterial routes.

2

VIRE, FRANCE

vaudeville

At its closest, the north coast of France is just twenty-one miles from the south coast of England. A byproduct of that geographical proximity is that over the past ten centuries England and France have found it all but impossible to resist the urge to invade one another. And at least one upshot of the greatest of all these invasions – the Norman Conquest of 1066 – is that roughly a third of the entire English language has its etymological roots on the opposite side of the Channel.

After his victory at the Battle of Hastings, the newly crowned King William I of England found it necessary to enforce his authority on his brand-new kingdom. As a consequence his native Norman French grew to become the dominant language of England's legal system, politics, finances and military. Latin remained the high-status language of the Church and education, but with French now installed as the language of the law and government in medieval England, the English language was relegated to bronze-medal position:* it became little more

---

* This Latin–French–English hierarchy still reverberates in our language today. Need a basic, straightforward word to get your message across? You're better off with something from the Anglo-Saxon end of the scale. Want something a little more formal? Try its French-origin synonym. On

than a day-to-day, low-status conversational language, used by an English-speaking population now translated into the unhappy subjects of a French-speaking king.

With so much business now being conducted in French, French-origin words naturally began to drift into the main-stream. Soon, English was awash with countless words and phrases imported by the victorious king and his attendant armies of ministers, bishops, knights, and – well, armies.

Words like *royal, sovereign, crown, duke* and *baron* began appear-ing in and around the king's court. *Judge, justice, jury, felony, verdict, bailiff* and *plaintiff* drifted into the language of the law, while the military now spoke of *armour, soldiers, archers, battles* and *guards*. This linguistic Norman invasion continued apace over the dec-ades that followed, leaving no corner of the language untouched, from the money we spend to the food we eat. So while the lowly Anglo-Saxons tended to their *pigs, sheep, cows* and *calves*, the ruling Normans enjoyed the fruits of their labour: the *pork*, the *mutton*, the *beef* and the *veal*.

That's not to say that William the Conqueror is single-handedly responsible for a third of your language being French, of course. It took several centuries for these and countless more words to become fully naturalised into our language. What's more, English being the magpie language that it is, it has unapologetically continued to pilfer words from its neighbour across *la Manche* ever since, including several of those whose origins lie on the French map.

the lookout for something with a little gravitas, useful only in the most specific of contexts? Then Latin is the way to go. That's why you might casually *ask* (Anglo-Saxon) someone what they got up to on their holi-days. But as soon as you start *questioning* (French) or *interrogating* them (Latin) on their holiday antics, the implications of your line of enquiry suddenly seem much more significant.

First on our itinerary is the picturesque town of Vire, roughly a hundred and fifty miles from Paris, in the rural west of Normandy. Vire has two somewhat infamous claims to fame. The first is that it ranks among the worst affected towns of the Second World War. On 6 June 1944, a relentless series of air raids unleashed a fire that raged so furiously the town's church bells melted and 95 per cent of its buildings were burned to the ground. Happily, Vire was not obliterated entirely from the map, and after the war it rose from the ashes to re-establish itself. Which is lucky, should you ever want to pay your respects to the founder of *vaudeville* theatre.

Vire's second claim to fame is that it was the birthplace of Olivier Basselin. Born around 1400, Basselin was a fuller by trade who operated a fabric mill alongside his wife on the outskirts of the town. But when he wasn't busy fulling cloth, Basselin apparently liked nothing more than dabbling in his two great interests: writing crude poems and drinking songs, and consuming enormous amounts of good-quality wine, and even better cider.

Alas, we don't know much more about Basselin and a great deal of what we do know has long since been shaped by centuries of lore and legend. But one thing we do know is that his crude songs and odes quickly proved popular, and before long much of sixteenth-century Normandy was singing along with what became known as his *chansons de vau-de-Vire* – his 'songs of the Vire valley'.

As the popularity of his songs spread, Basselin's bawdy style came to be imitated by other writers and performers, and this *vau-de-Vire* repertoire began to swell; by 1610, a local lawyer named Jean Le Houx had accumulated enough material to publish an anthology of Basselin's and his contemporaries' work.*

---

* As a telling indictment of the precise content of these songs, on publication of his *Le Livre des Chants nouveaux de Vaudevire*, Le Houx reportedly

But just as the popularity of these songs reached its peak, their etymological connection with their home town began to fade.

By the time Le Houx's anthology was published, Basselin's *vau-de-Vire* had morphed into a single word, *vaudevire*. Confusion with *ville*, the French for 'town', soon ensued, and before long these entertainments had come to be known by an entirely new name: *vaudeville*.

That word finally made its debut in English in the mid seventeenth century, by which point its connection both to Vire and to Basselin had been relegated to the footnotes:

> *Vaudeville: A country ballade, or song; a roundelay or virelay;*
> *so termed of Vaudevire, a Norman town, wherein Olivier Bassel*
> *[sic], the first inventor of them, lived.*
> —Thomas Blount, *Glossographia* (1656)

The word had changed, but as time went by so too did the entertainment itself. By the eighteenth century, *vaudeville* songs were no longer bawdy accompaniments to drunken binges, but light popular ditties and music-hall numbers, often with comic or satirical edges. By the nineteenth century, they had found their way into English and American theatres and playhouses, where they were joined on stage by an assortment of magicians, tumblers, comedians, strongmen, actors and impersonators. Ultimately, by the turn of the century, *vaudeville* had become a catch-all term for any kind of variety performance.

As for Basselin, rumour has it that he died fighting the English in the Battle of Formigny in 1450, one of the final battles of the Hundred Years War.

Another skirmish between the English and the French, you say? Surely not . . .

travelled from Normandy to Rome to seek absolution merely for the sin of editing the book.

3

SAVERNE, FRANCE

zabernism

From Normandy, we head four hundred miles east to Alsace, the ancient region on the west bank of the Rhine sandwiched between modern-day France and Germany.

As the fertile borderland between two of Europe's greatest (and historically most bellicose) superpowers, ownership of Alsace has long been hard fought. It is prime European real estate – the geographical equivalent of the last slice of pizza – eyed up by ravenous tribes, dynasties, states and empires for centuries, and either snatched without apology or politely passed on.

From the Romans (who first laid claim to the region in the first century BCE) to the Germanic *Alemanni* tribe (who picked up where the Romans left off) to the Franks (who seized control at the Battle of Tolbiac in 496), Alsace continued to change hands, rarely without a fight, right through to the collapse of the region's Nazi annexation in 1945. And this long war-torn history is reflected not only in Alsace's distinctive language and culture, but by the battle-scarred stories behind many of the words the region has inspired.

During the Thirty Years War, 1618–48, Alsace found itself on the battlefront between the territorially ambitious Protestant armies of central and northern Europe, and the equally ambitious

Catholic armies of the south and west. The war came to an end with the Treaty of Westphalia, which handed control of Alsace (albeit temporarily) back to France. But by then the conflict had taken such a toll that many of the region's people had either fled or been killed, and as a consequence France imposed relatively little authority over it. All but ignored by the rest of the country, it came to be repopulated by an inharmonious mix of displaced and exiled peoples, each with their own cultures, priorities and notions of what was best for the future of the region. Before long, Alsace had slipped into an uneasy period of divided self-governance and widespread misrule.

France finally stepped in to establish full sovereignty in Alsace in 1681, but by then its reputation for lawlessness had become legendary, and *Alsatia* – the Latin name for Alsace – had morphed into a byword for any lawless or anarchic place, or anywhere operating as an ungovernable safe haven for criminals and miscreants. In English slang in particular, *Alsatia* became a cant nickname for the London precinct of Whitefriars, which had long been home to a Carmelite monastery with right of sanctuary, acting as asylum to an unruly assembly of rogues and petty thieves, outlaws, prostitutes, murderers and wrongdoers of all kinds:

> *White-Friars at London was a sanctuary . . . called Alsatia; thither many broken and disorderly persons repaired. They invented for themselves a sort of gibberish vulgarly termed Alsatian Cant. It must be acknowledged to the disgrace of our country, that some words issuing from that mint did obtain currency, and that people of quality came to use the dialect of whores and sharpers.* *
> — *The Edinburgh Magazine, or Literary Miscellany* (1788)

---

* The English playwright Thomas Shadwell satirised this state of affairs in his 1688 comedy *The Squire of Alsatia*, the preface to which included a

That Latin name, *Alsatia*, is also unsurprisingly the origin of the name of the *Alsatian* dog. But surely one the world's most popular and charismatic dog breeds can't have a tale of military unrest in its history too? Well . . .

Credit for the very first Alsatian dog, from which all others are now descended, goes to Hektor Linksrhein, or Horand von Grafrath as he was also known. Oddly those aren't the names of some venerated German dog-breeder, but the actual canine forefather in question: born in 1895, Hektor was four years old when he was exhibited at a dog show in Frankfurt in 1899, where he happened to catch the eye of one Max Emil von Stephanitz. Stephanitz (it's probably worth pointing out) was not a dog, but rather a former German cavalry officer and veterinarian, who had spent much of the 1890s working to establish a standardised national German breed of dog. Impressed by Hektor's strength, stamina and intelligence, Stephanitz paid the princely sum of 200 marks for him, renamed him Horand, and established a breeding programme that saw him father litter after litter of puppies, each carrying its fair share of their father's superlative genetic make-up.

Stephanitz named this new breed the *Deutscher Schäferhund*, or 'German shepherd-dog', a nod both to the dog's homeland, and to the so-called 'Continental shepherd-dog' from which he presumed it had evolved. The breed soon proved popular, both as a working dog and as household pet, but just as Hektor and his offspring began to reach the peak of their popularity in the early 1900s, war once more erupted across Europe.

glossary of local cant. So should you ever feel the need to disgrace your country and imitate a whore or a sharper, feel free to call your clothes your *rigging*; your watch your *tattler*; a gullible or easily duped person a *putt*; and a habitual cheat a *tattmonger*. If you're *rhinocerical*, then you're flush with cash, while if you're *blowsy* or *clear*, in Shadwell's terms, then you're either 'drunk' or 'very drunk'.

For four years, the continent was torn apart by one of the bloodiest conflicts in human history. By the time fighting ceased, four great empires had fallen, maps and borders had been redrawn, 35 million soldiers and civilians lay dead, and a widespread distaste for all things German had enveloped the Western world. Post-1918, anything or anyone bearing a German name or exhibiting even the slightest hint of German heritage fell victim to increasingly toxic anti-German sentiment.

Sauerkraut was one of the earliest and most famous casualties of this war on words, finding itself renamed 'liberty cabbage' in American stores and restaurants. *Hamburgers* likewise became 'liberty steaks' and *frankfurters* became 'liberty sausages'. Even *German measles* began to be re-diagnosed as 'liberty measles'. The questionably named towns of Berlin and Germania in Iowa, and Germantown in Nebraska, rebranded themselves as 'Lincoln', 'Lakota', and 'Garland' respectively. And even the British royal family wasn't exempt: in 1917, George V felt compelled to sweep his household's ancestry under the rug at Sandringham House, issuing a proclamation that changed their dynastic name from Saxe-Coburg-Gotha to the decidedly more English-sounding 'Windsor'.

Naturally, it did not take long for the judgemental eye of this anti-German scrutiny to fall on the newly named *German shepherd*. In 1917, the American Kennel Club dropped the word 'German' from the breed's name, and began registering all new puppies merely as 'shepherd dogs'. But in the UK, the club went a step further: in 1919, it adopted an entirely new name for the breed emphasising its likely origins among domesticated wolves on the French–German border. The 'Alsatian wolf-dog', as it was first known, had finally arrived.

Happily, this anti-German feeling did not endure. Despite the tumult of the Second World War, by the mid 1970s several campaigns had successfully lobbied the Kennel Club into dropping this outdated euphemism and reinstating the breed's original

name. The first 'German shepherd' in fifty-eight years was registered in 1977, and although the term remains in popular use
among owners and breeders today, the name *Alsatian* was finally
dropped from the Kennel Club's register altogether in 2010.

But before we pack our bags and head across the border
on the next leg of our journey, Alsace has one more war-torn
etymological tale to tell – this one hidden away in the very final
pages of the dictionary.

Coined in the early 1900s, *zabernism* is the overzealous use or
abuse of military power; to *zabernise*, likewise, is to bully or antag-
onise with military force. At the root of this linguistic curio is the
Alsatian town of Saverne, thirty miles from Strasbourg, which in
1913 became the unlikely setting for a scandal of military heavy-
handedness that would eventually throw all of Germany into a
constitutional crisis.

At the time of the affair Alsace was part of the German
empire, as it had been ever since France relinquished the territory following the Franco–Prussian War in 1871. Saverne was
now a major Prussian garrison town known by its German name,
Zabern, while Alsace was now officially the German Imperial
Territory of Alsace-Lorraine, a province under the direct rule of
the Kaiser, some five hundred miles away in Berlin.

Alsace has always had close cultural ties to its German neighbours, but at the time many people resented this forced return to
German imperial rule* – especially with France's ever strengthening appetite for republicanism and parliamentary democracy
only a stone's throw away. The German response to all this

---

* Signed on 10 May 1871, one of the constituent clauses of the Treaty
of Frankfurt, which officially ended the Franco–Prussian War, gave the
citizens of Alsace a deadline of 1 October the following year to decide
whether to leave Alsace and emigrate to France, or to remain where they
were and become German citizens. Some 160,000 people – almost 10 per
cent of the population – opted to retain French citizenship.

resentment was predictably heavy-handed: regional identity in Alsace was suppressed, with the use of both the French and native Alsatian languages all but prohibited. The response in Alsace, meanwhile, was largely defiant: with Germany wanting their ties to France inhibited, the Alsatians responded by circulating several new French- and Alsatian-language journals and periodicals.

By the 1910s, the people of Alsace had endured four decades of this uncomfortable German rule, and although Germany finally granted Alsace some autonomy in 1911 (allowing it to adopt its own constitution, flag and national anthem), these tokenistic gestures did little to quell the growing discontent. Before long, Alsace had become an uneasy powder keg of unrest, with only the slightest provocation needed to provide the spark. On 28 October 1913, that spark came in the form of a young Prussian soldier named Günter von Forstner.

Forstner was a hot-headed twenty-year-old lieutenant in the Prussian Army, who, despite his age, had already acquired a reputation as a bully and braggart among his fellow soldiers; on one occasion, he had reportedly struck down an Alsatian cobbler in the streets of Zabern for no reason other than that he had failed to acknowledge Forstner properly as he had walked by. On the morning in question, Forstner was overseeing a troop induction exercise at the Zabern garrison when a scuffle broke out among some of the new recruits. As he ran to break up the fight, Forstner angrily exclaimed that if it was a fight the recruits were looking for, they should go out into the town and pick a fight with a *Wackes* – a hugely derogatory German slur (derived from the same root as *vagabond*) for a citizen of Alsace.

Wackes was such a highly charged word that its use among members of the German Army had been banned in 1903. Not content with using it only once, Forstner continued his tirade. Should a fight break out in the town, he went on, then the recruits should not think twice about using their weapons, and he would personally pay 10 marks for every *Wackes* they killed.

His remarks, understandably, were incendiary, and when news reached the local press, a thousand-strong crowd[*] of protestors – many shouting, '*Vive la France!*' – gathered outside the garrison. The German reaction, however, could scarcely have been worse: the authorities at first tried to play down the episode (even going so far as to question precisely how insulting a term *Wackes* really was), while Forstner's superiors held back from reprimanding him for his insensitivity, and instead turned their attention to the handful of Alsatian recruits they suspected had leaked his words to the press. The recruits were arrested, the offices of a local newspaper were illegally raided, and unrest in the town reached a fever pitch.

Amid mounting pressure, Forstner was finally disciplined and placed under six days' house arrest, but news of this reprimand failed to be reported to the people of Zabern, who wrongly presumed his actions had still gone unpunished. So when his detention was over and he returned to active duty, Forstner was still met with jeers and harassment on the streets of Zabern (as well as being the subject of the indelible and decidedly unpleasant rumour that after a particularly wild night on the drink, he had returned to his bed at the garrison, passed out in a drunken stupor, and promptly soiled himself). The relationship between the people of Zabern and the German Army had never been worse, but Forstner, now the despised laughing stock of the town, was not done yet.

Two weeks after his initial comments, Forstner's inability to hold his tongue soon threw him back into the fray. Now back on duty, he casually explained to another group of recruits that should they have any thoughts of deserting and joining the French Foreign Legion, they could go and 'shit on the French

---

[*] Not a bad turnout for a town of just 8,000 people.

flag' for all he cared. Once more, his behaviour had proved incendiary. News of Forstner's crude jibe quickly spread far outside the garrison, and soon even further beyond the borders of Alsace. Before long, the eyes of France – and eventually those of the entire Western world – were turned to Zabern, as world leaders nervously awaited Germany's response to the scandal and the mounting unrest in the town. A recommendation was made to the Kaiser back in Berlin for Forstner to be transferred to avoid risking any further gaffes and to defuse the situation as painlessly as possible. But the Kaiser, not wanting to see his military back down in the eyes of the people, refused: Forstner remained at his post, the protestors remained outside the garrison gates, and for a time the scandal rumbled on. Until, finally, enough was enough. With Zabern now under international scrutiny, on 30 November 1913, Forstner's commanding officer, Colonel von Reuter, took it on himself to suppress the unrest in the town once and for all.

Reuter ordered sixty German soldiers, Forstner among them, to take up their rifles, fix bayonets, and march with him out into the town square. This show of strength, he wagered, would soon put the people of the town back in their place. So, with drums beating, and two machine guns hauled out alongside them, Reuter and his men entered the square and confronted the crowd.

The response from the townspeople was one of stunned disbelief. Those merely going about their everyday business stopped in their tracks, while those who had been protesting outside the garrison jeered, whistled and even laughed at Reuter's ludicrously overblown show of force. He was furious. With, as he later recalled, the 'prestige and honour of the whole army' now at stake, he ordered the arrest of anyone 'who stood still even for a second' in the town square. The soldiers advanced, and total chaos ensued.

Anyone and everyone who happened to be in the square now found themselves a suspect accused of dishonouring the

German Army. A banker returning home from work was arrested for smiling. A young man was arrested for singing. A company of judges exiting a nearby courthouse found themselves caught up in the commotion and thrown in jail for nothing more than standing still too long, as they looked on in disbelief at the pandemonium before them. In all, twenty-seven arrests were made, most for the very slightest of transgressions; when challenged on this heavy-handed and largely unnecessary show of strength, Reuter merely replied, 'I am in command here now.'

The response to the events in Zabern that day was one of profound shock. Editorials the world over called into question not only Forstner's, and now Reuter's, actions, but those of the entire German military, who, according to the *New York Tribune*, had ominously started to 'regard themselves not so much the servants of the state, but as the overlords of all mere civilians'. Back in Berlin, questions were raised in the Reichstag over the ability of the military to act as a police force; over who had the authority to challenge and police the military themselves; and over the rights of local people and local courts to stand against the military and enforce their own jurisdiction. A long-forgotten law from the days of the Napoleonic Wars, which permitted the military, under siege conditions, to quell riots when the local authorities failed to act, was hauled out of the history books and put under the constitutional microscope. Had the military in Zabern violated their constitutional limits? Had Reuter acted appropriately under strained circumstances? Question after question was raised and debated, but with little resolution. Eventually, facing a growing constitutional crisis and a vote of no confidence, the German Chancellor withdrew the entire garrison from Zabern. But to appease those in his parliament who had supported the military's response, only the lightest of punishments were meted out to those involved. Although questions still remained unanswered and anger still raged, the outbreak of the First World War in 1914 abruptly ended the debate. The snowballing Zabern Affair had at long last come to a close.

By then, however, news of the crisis had spread far and wide, and *zabernism*, the overzealous use of military power or authority (or 'military jackbootery' as one 1921 dictionary defined it) had found its way into the language. The word has remained in occasional use – and, alas, has remained occasionally useful – ever since.

4

SPA, BELGIUM

spa

With three tales of war and warfare behind us, we leave France and head north into a country without which we'd have no saxophones, no contraceptive pills, no inline skates, no Brussels sprouts, and, oddly, no French fries.*

* The origin of the French fry is subject to a lengthy dispute between France and Belgium, with the Belgians claiming that peasants in the Meuse valley were frying chopped potatoes in oil as early as the seventeenth century. The saxophone, meanwhile, was invented by Belgian musician Adolphe Sax in 1846, and the science behind the modern oral contraceptive pill is credited to Nand Peeters, an obstetrician and gynaecologist born in Mechelen in 1918. As well as giving the world an early form of self-propelled wheelchair and a pedal-operated revolving tea-table, Belgian inventor John Joseph Merlin is credited with producing the very first inline skates in 1760. Alas, while demonstrating his 'skates contrived to run on wheels' and simultaneously playing the violin at Carlisle House in London in the late 1700s, Merlin, 'not having provided the means of retarding his velocity, or commanding its direction . . . impelled himself against a mirror of more than £500 value, dashed it to atoms, broke his instrument to pieces, and wounded himself most severely'.

But that's not all we owe to our North Sea neighbours in Belgium. (The humble sprout is by no means the only word in the dictionary to have taken its name from the Belgian map.) Without Belgium, we'd have no weekends away at health *spas*. Worse still, Paddington Bear would be without his trademark *duffel* coat.

Duffel is the name of a small town south of Antwerp, where a thick woollen fabric bearing the town's name has been produced since the fifteenth century at least. Before long, this durable, heavy-duty cloth was being used to manufacture all kinds of hard-wearing items, from blankets and coverlets to thick weatherproof overcoats and equally thick, equally weatherproof backpacks and satchels. By the nineteenth century, its popularity had spread worldwide, and duffel cloth had become so synonymous with these hard-wearing bags that the word *duffel* was being used for any military-style sack made of heavy-duty fabric. In American English in particular, an anglicised version, *duffle*, had become a byword for the random kit and equipment kept inside a duffel bag – as mentioned in this crucial piece of advice from a nineteenth-century guide to the great outdoors:

> *When the winter rains are making out-of-door life unbearable [in the woods] . . . it is well that a few congenial spirits should, at some favourite trysting place, gather around the glowing stove and exchange yarns, opinions and experiences. Perhaps no two will exactly agree on the best ground for an outing . . . But one thing all admit. Each and every one has gone to his chosen ground with too much impedimenta, too much duffle . . . The temptation to buy this or that bit of indispensable camp-kit has been too strong and we have gone to the blessed woods handicapped with a load fit for a pack-mule. This is not how you do it.*
> —George Washington Sears, *Woodcraft & Camping* (1884)

No, that is not how you do it. But that is how you warn others against taking too much kit.

Eighty miles from Duffel is another Belgian town whose name has found its way into the dictionary – although linguistic folklore would have you believe otherwise.

There's an old etymological legend that claims the word *spa* is an acronym for the Latin tag *sanitas per aquam*, or 'health through water'. But just like the equally tall tales behind words like *posh*, *golf*, and *cabal** (and just like that dubious theory about potentially explosive manure once being '*shipped high in transit*'), in reality there's no acronym hiding here. *Spa* merely derives from the Belgian town of Spa, whose natural mineral waters were once so well known across Europe that its name became a byword for any similar resort.

Spa stands in a valley in the Ardennes mountains, where a number of thermal freshwater springs have bubbled up to the surface to provide the town with both a continual supply of mineral-rich water and a continual supply of cash-rich tourists, who have for centuries been drawn to the supposedly curative waters.

Writing in the first century CE, the Roman scholar Pliny the Elder was among the first to describe a 'remarkable spring that sparkles with innumerable bubbles' in the Belgian corner of Gaul, which contained, he advised, health-giving waters that could be used as a 'purgative' and as a cure for 'three-day fevers', bladder stones and other 'calculous affections'. Quite how effective a remedy the waters actually proved is debatable, but no matter: tales of their healing and invigorating properties

---

* Legend has it that five members of Charles II's inner sanctum – Lord Clifford, the Earl of Arlington, the Duke of Buckingham, Lord Ashley and the Duke of Lauderdale – gave their names to Charles's so-called Cabal Ministry, and ultimately gave us the word *cabal*. They didn't. *Cabal* comes via Latin from *qabbalah*, a Hebrew word for a traditional interpretation of the Old Testament.

continued to circulate, and before long Spa was attracting quite the A-list clientele.

Augustine de Augustinus, a Venetian-born physician who counted both Henry VIII and Cardinal Wolsey among his patients, is said to have been one of Spa's earliest foreign advocates. So too were Margaret of Valois, wife of Henry IV of France, and the English king Charles II, who visited Spa's thermal baths during his exile in 1654. Even Russia's Peter the Great got in on the act, labelling Spa 'the best place to take the waters' in all of Europe.

Others, admittedly, were less impressed. When the Italian adventurer Giacomo Casanova found himself in Spa in the summer of 1783, he mused, 'I don't know by what convention, once a year, every summer, all nations of Europe assemble [*here*] to do all sorts of foolish things.' (Finding no female interest in the town other than 'an English lady who . . . addressed me with proposals that froze me with fear', he quickly moved on.) The poet Matthew Arnold likewise complained that Spa 'astonished us by its insignificance' when he visited in 1860, but by then the town had become something of a victim of its own success.

It was during its heyday in the mid eighteenth century that Spa became so celebrated internationally that its name became a nickname for any similar health resort; the earliest use of *spa* in this context dates from 1781. But by then so many visitors were plaguing the town that a 'cure tax' was imposed in an attempt to discourage their numbers – with little effect. And with the visitors came the visitor attractions.

Shops, hotels, restaurants, casinos and even an opera house were all constructed in Spa in an effort to cash in on the tourists' francs, transforming it from a serene, picturesque mountain retreat into a bustling honeytrap and a luxury playground for the wealthy and well connected. As similar 'spa resorts' began to emerge elsewhere, Spa failed to see off the competition and its popularity began to dwindle. The town continued to struggle during the two world wars and the post-war decades, and eventually saw out the twentieth century a shadow of its former self.

Recent attempts to revive the town have proved successful and have sparked a resurgence in tourism, but no matter what its prospects may be, the town's place in etymological history – and, for that matter, in our dictionary – has long since been secured.

5

NEANDER VALLEY, GERMANY

Neanderthal

From a valley in the Ardennes we head eighty miles across the Belgian border, to a valley on the River Düssel in western Germany.

Admittedly, a former limestone quarry on the outskirts of Düsseldorf might not sound like the most exciting destination on a round-the-world voyage. And that's because it isn't. But bear with me: Germany's Neander valley has more than earned its place on our itinerary, as in the mid nineteenth century it was the site of a discovery that would not only earn it a place in our language, but change our understanding of human history forever.

This particular story begins twenty metres up the wall of a gorge in the Neander Valley, in a small cave known locally as the Kleine Feldhofer Grotte.

One morning in August 1856, two quarrymen ascended the side of the gorge and began to excavate the cave's floor, removing a thick deposit of hardened clay that had set over the valuable limestone below. But as they worked, their pickaxes suddenly struck bone, not rock. First the top of a skull, then a pair of thigh bones, a few arm bones, and finally some fragments of ribs and a shoulder blade all slowly emerged out of the earth.

It sounds like quite the find, but uncovering bones was par for the course in excavations like these, and the men's discovery was promptly dismissed as nothing more than the worthless remains of a cave bear, or some other ancient animal. Thinking little more of it, they tossed the bones onto a pile of debris and carried on with their work. Luckily for us, however, that's not where this story ends.

Word of the bones soon reached Wilhelm Beckershoff, the owner of the cave, and Friedrich Wilhelm Pieper, the owner of the mine. Curious to know what creature they had belonged to, the pair contacted a local schoolteacher and amateur naturalist named Johann Carl Fuhlrott, who visited the site to investigate. He instantly recognised that because they had been found fossilised beneath two solid feet of mud, they must belong to some very ancient creature indeed. But, even more important, they appeared to be human.

Fuhlrott gathered the remaining fragments together and took them to Hermann Schaaffhausen, professor of anatomy at the University of Bonn. Schaaffhausen's expertise proved invaluable: he was able to note several subtle differences – the domed oval cranium, the prominent tapering browline, the low, apelike forehead – between these bones and ordinary human remains.

A year of painstaking research and analysis followed, until finally he and Fuhlrott came to an astonishing conclusion: the bones found in the cave must have belonged to a member of some ancient race of early humans, who likely roamed Europe sometime during the last Ice Age.

Fuhlrott and Schaafferhausen's theory stunned and divided the scientific community in equal measure. At the time (a full two years before the publication of Darwin's *Origin of Species*) many people were not prepared to believe that such proto-humans had ever existed, and rejected all but a biblical explanation of the origin of man.* Many were ultimately left to concoct ever more unlikely explanations of their own to reconcile their religious beliefs with Schaaffhausen's compelling anatomical evidence. The bones, some said, were those of some long-dead Cossack cavalryman whose lifetime of horse riding explained the strong, bowed thigh bones. Others claimed they must have belonged to some misshapen sufferer of rickets who had died in exile, while the heavy receding brow must have been formed by near-constant frowning and grimacing caused by pain from a badly healed fracture in one of the arms. Every last pathological straw was thoroughly clutched in an effort to discredit Fuhlrott and Schaaffhausen's conclusion, but to no avail. As similarities between their find and other humanlike remains found elsewhere in Europe began to be observed, the wider scientific community steadily warmed to their remarkable conclusion.

Finally, in 1863, the influential Irish geologist William King proposed once and for all that the Feldhofer bones, and those of other specimens like it, belonged not only to some ancient archaic human but to a member of an entirely distinct species. King gave this species the name *Homo neanderthalenis*, literally 'man of the Neander Valley', and we've acknowledged our distant *Neanderthal* cousins ever since.

From *frankfurters* to *Black Forest gateaux*, and from *homburgs* (a style of hat named after Homburg, near Wiesbaden) to *hamburgers* (named after Hamburg, not because they're made of ham), German towns and cities have contributed a lot more to our

---

* Ironically, this discovery – which shook the erstwhile unshakeable nineteenth-century belief in Christian creationism – took place in a valley named in honour of a devout Calvinist theologian and hymn-writer. Joachim Neander (1650–1680) delivered sermons and held religious services in the valley while working as a schoolteacher and minister in Düsseldorf in the late 1600s. After his death, the valley that he had so admired was named in his honour.

language than the name of an ancient hominid. The dictionary also lists a number of light-hearted (if somewhat less welcome) German-inspired words and phrases.

A *German comb*, for instance, was nineteenth-century slang for the fingers of a hand run through a person's hair. A *German duck*, for some long-forgotten reason, was a bed louse. And a *German goitre* is a bulging belly – a reference to the fine quality and bloatingly high calorific content of German beer. But when it comes to unwelcome etymological connotations, the next stop on our journey fares among the worst in the language.

6

AMSTERDAM, NETHERLANDS

ampster

B ritain and the Netherlands, historically two of the world's greatest seafaring nations, have long been close allies with a lengthy history of kinship and peaceful cooperation. Apart from the Anglo-Dutch War, of course. And the Second Anglo-Dutch War that broke out a decade after that. And, for that matter, the Third Anglo-Dutch War the decade after that. But apart from *those*, the two countries have always got along. Although there was the Fourth Anglo-Dutch War in 1780. And relations weren't great during the Glorious Revolution either, when the Dutch prince William of Orange overthrew James II and claimed the English throne. And then, of course, Britain fought against Dutch troops during the French Revolutionary War. And the Napoleonic Wars too. Hmm. Is it too late to start this chapter again? Right.

Britain and the Netherlands have a long history of mutual enmity and have declared war on one another countless times throughout their combined histories. And for precisely that reason, all things Dutch don't come off too well when you look them up in the dictionary.

Probably the most famous example of this anti-Dutch senti-ment* is the English expression *Dutch courage* – namely, not true courage at all, but temporary bravery occasioned by alcohol. Then there's *double Dutch*, a nineteenth-century expression allud-ing to the fact that English speakers once found spoken Dutch so unintelligible that its name became a byword for impenetrable gibberish. *Dutch jawbreakers*, likewise, are words deemed impos-sibly difficult to pronounce, and in sixteenth-century English, *Dutch fustian* was impossibly overblown or pretentiously impen-etrable language (though more on that later).

A *Dutch auction* is an auction in which a high opening price has to be lowered until it attracts the first bidder. In eighteenth-century English, a *Dutch concert* was cacophonous sound of more than one song or piece of music being performed simultaneously. A *Dutch bargain* is no bargain at all, but a deal in which one side takes advantage of the other. And when a carpenter goes to hit a nail but misses, the resulting indentation is nicknamed a *Dutch rose*.

To do a Dutch is to desert one's responsibilities. To offer *Dutch consolation* is to be thankful that things aren't any worse than they already are. A *Dutch widow* was once a prostitute, and a *Dutch clock* a bedpan. To take a *Dutchman's draught* is to unapologetically take the last swig from a shared bottle – the kind of brazen behaviour you might expect from the host of a *Dutch feast*, a slang expres-sion for a party at which the host gets drunk before the guests. A *Dutchman's anchor* is anything that, when desperately needed, cannot be found; according to Frank C. Bowen's 1929 collection of *Sea Slang*, this term alludes to an infamous Dutch sea captain,

---

* Perhaps unsurprisingly, this is a two-way street. To the Dutch, 'to write an English letter', *een Engelschen brief schrijven*, is to take a nap after eating a large meal, and a reputation for poor English diets and endless epidemics likewise led to sweating sickness being known as *Engelsch zweet*, or 'English sweat', and rickets as *Engelsche ziekte*, or 'English disease'.

'who explained after the wreck that he had a very good anchor, but had left it at home'. And perhaps strangest of all, according to one dictionary of 1912, 'when a person treads in dung, he is said to cut his foot with a Dutchman's razor'.

With all of these in mind, it might come as little surprise to discover that the name of the capital of the Netherlands, *Amsterdam* – or *ampster* for short – is an old slang word for a con artist's accomplice, or a plant placed in the audience of a show-boating pedlar to encourage the crowd to buy whatever he's hawking. It might sound as if we should add this word to that long list of anti-Dutch expressions above, but, bucking the trend here, there is actually a much more wholesome explanation.

According to the *Oxford English Dictionary*, *ampster* probably first emerged in Australian English, and derives not from the English language's age-old animosity towards the Dutch but from Australian rhyming slang. An *Amsterdam*, among Australian sheep farmers at least, is a ram, and perhaps because of the questionable behaviour of rutting male sheep, it was the word *ram* that initially became a slang nickname for a fraudster's assistant. The words eventually became conflated, however, and *Amsterdam* was reluctantly dragged into an unwholesome association with tricksters and underhand dealings in the early 1940s. Sometimes etymology really isn't fair.

7

COPENHAGEN,
DENMARK

Great Dane

We now double back through Germany and travel onwards, northwards, into Scandinavia.

It's a funny word, *Scandinavia*. Etymologically, its roots lie in an Old Norse name for the southernmost region of Sweden, *Skáney*, to which has been added an ancient Germanic word meaning 'island'. Put together, that gave us a Germanic name for the far north of Europe something along the lines of *Scadinauja* – or, at least, that was until the Ancient Roman scholar and author Pliny the Elder got his hands on it.

In his *Natural History* (c. 79 CE), Pliny described several of the creatures that originate 'in the North Parts' of Europe, including among them the elk, 'maned bisons', several 'remarkable kinds of wild cattle', and a curious creature he called the *machlis*:

> *In Scandinavia, but nowhere else in the world, there is a beast called the Machlis, not much unlike [the elk] ... but without any bending of the pastern, and therefore he never lieth down but sleepeth leaning against a tree ... Their upper lip is exceeding*

great, and therefore as they feed they go backward; for if they passed forward, it would be folded double.
—Pliny the Elder, *Natural History* (XIII.xvi)

Now, it's fair to say Pliny wasn't particularly well known for his scientific accuracy even at the best of times. (After all, it was he who gave us the myth that ostriches bury their heads in the sand, and elsewhere in his *Natural History* he talks of a race of dog-headed people who bark at each other, and another whose feet are so large they can lie on their backs and shade themselves from the sun.) And he makes a fair few factual missteps here too.

For one, he thought the fabled '*machlis*' was a different creature from the elk. It wasn't – *machlis* was just another name for it. Secondly, elk are perfectly capable of lying down, and certainly don't need to lean against a tree to fall asleep. And nor do they have such fleshy lips that if they were to graze while walking forwards they wouldn't be able to eat. And nor, oddly enough, did they live in Pliny's 'Scandinavia': somehow, Pliny managed to drop an extra N into the existing name *Scadinavia*, and thanks to the popularity and influence of his work after his death, it's remained with us ever since.

But Pliny's *Scandinavia* isn't the only etymological malfunction the north of Europe has to offer. While we're staying here in Denmark, there's one more misstep worth pointing out.

Denmark's contributions to the dictionary range from *Danish pastries* (first mentioned in English in the 1910s) to *Danish embroidery* (an especially fine style of needlework) and *Denmark satin* (a high-quality fabric once used to make Victorian women's shoes). Each is a world leader in its respective field[*] and ultimately namechecks its country of origin with considerable pride.

[*] As a world leader both in medicine and in liberal attitudes, Denmark is also namechecked in the expression *to go to Denmark* – 1960s slang for undertaking gender reassignment surgery. The phrase is a reference to

As, for that matter, does the *Great Dane* – another world leader, holding as it does the record for the world's tallest dog. But while the Great Dane has always been *great*, it hasn't always been – well, a *Dane*.

Genetically, the Great Dane's origins are thought to lie among the fierce hunters' hounds of Ancient Greece. Over centuries, these ferocious boarhounds spread across Europe, where they were bred and crossbred with various other breeds – including greyhounds, English mastiffs and Irish wolfhounds – to produce ever more sizeable, tenacious and intelligent dogs. By the sixteenth century, the breed as we know it today had started to emerge in what is now Germany: in 1592, the Duke of Braunschweig reportedly assembled a pack of 600 exclusively male dogs for a boar hunt on his estate (which tells you a little something of the size of his estate, and rather a lot more about how badly it must have smelled). But while these grand dogs were certainly among the modern Great Dane's genetic ancestors, they were by no means among their etymological ones.

Thanks to the popularity of long-legged English and Irish breeds in the quest for ever taller and ever more powerful hunting hounds, these early hybrids became known in their native German as *Englischer Hundes*, or 'English dogs'. As the breed continued to standardise over the years that followed, national pride took over, so that by the nineteenth century these 'English dogs' had been rebranded *Deutsche Dogges*, or 'German dogs'; an official Deutsche Dogge Club of Germany was founded in 1891. The breed's German connection endured even outside Germany: in France, it became known as the *dogue allemande*, in Spain it was the *alano alemán*, and in English it was originally the *German boarhound*. But around the turn of the century, all that began to change.

Christine Jorgensen, a New York-born trans woman who travelled to Denmark in 1951 to undergo a much-publicised procedure.

As tension between Germany and its neighbours began to heat up, ultimately – just as it had done with the *Alsatian* – the appetite for anything and everything sounding even vaguely German evaporated. As a result credit for these tall and robust hunting hounds was snatched from Germany and handed to its northern neighbour, Denmark: by the early twentieth century, the *German boarhound* had successfully been rebranded in the English-speaking world as the *Great Dane*.

Quite why Denmark should have been given the credit is unclear, but it is likely that the new name was meant to have harked back to an earlier breed that had become popular in the 1700s under the French name *grand danois*. Whatever the explanation, it's all a geographical miscellany: from Ancient Greece to not-quite-so-ancient Germany, by way of England and Ireland, and eventually handed, rather unceremoniously, to Denmark. The *Great Dane* really isn't all that Danish.

8

OSLO, NORWAY

Oslo breakfast

From Denmark, we head due north across the waters of the Skagerrak and on to Norway.

Admittedly, not many names from the Norwegian map have found their way into our language. But one of the few that has is ominously described here:

> *The principallest and most perilous of all [dangerous places in the sea] is the Maelstream Well, or Slorp . . . which lieth on the backside of Norway . . . This well draweth the water into itself . . . with such an in-draught and force, and with such a noise through the tumbling and falling of the waves . . . no ship or other vessel may come near, for they should to their utter destruction be drawn into it and swallowed up.*
> —A. Ashley, *The Mariner's Mirrour* (1588)

Sadly, we're not talking about the word *slorp* here. Nor are we talking about the expression *backside of Norway*. To the navigators and seafarers of the sixteenth century, the violent Norwegian whirlpool described here bore the name *maelstrom*. And it's from there – a Dutch-origin word literally meaning 'grinding stream' – that we've since acquired a word for any violently turbulent situation.

The original *maelstrom* from which all others derive their names is now known as the Moskstraumen, and rather than appear as a single swirling vortex as in the account above, it is in truth a vast and powerful system of inter-spiralling tidal eddies that lies off the coast of (and takes its name from) Moskenesøya island, in Norway's Lofoten archipelago. The name *maelstrom* might not exist on maps today but its ancient equivalent at least survives in the dictionary. But it's not a perilous whirlpool that has brought us to Norway.

With Denmark now behind us there are no *Danish pastries* on the menu: here in Norway, the second of our Scandinavian stop-offs, it's time for an *Oslo breakfast*.

If you're craving something hearty, you might be disappointed. An *Oslo breakfast* comprises two slices of wholemeal bread and margarine, a single sausage or slice of whey cheese, half an apple (or, if you want to go all out, half an orange) and a half-pint glass of fresh milk. Still not full? Well, you're in luck: according to Carl Schiøtz, the Norwegian nutritionist who pioneered the *Oslo breakfast* regime in the late 1920s, you can add a single raw carrot to your morning spread should you wish, and (albeit during the winter months only) you can wash it all down with a nice healthful dose of cod liver oil.

Frankly, it's not quite a bacon sandwich. But by the mid 1930s this *Oslo breakfast* was being served to every schoolchild in the city, and by the 1940s the regime had proved so successful that it had been adopted and implemented in several other cities and countries around the world. Moreover, the term *Oslo breakfast*, or *Oslo meal*, had earned itself a permanent place in our dictionary – both in reference to Schiøtz's original dietary scheme, and as a looser term for any wholesome and nutritious start to the day. But how did such a seemingly meagre meal come to gain worldwide attention?

This story begins in Oslo (or Kristiania, as it was at the time) at the end of the nineteenth century. The city authorities had begun serving free hot school meals to children in Oslo in the late 1800s, but by the turn of the century food scientists had started to cast doubt on quite how nutritious and sustaining these free meals were.

In 1927, into this nutritional debate stepped Professor Carl Schiøtz, whose academic work had long focused on the role of nutrition in childhood. Using the most up-to-date data he could find, Schiøtz compiled the menu outlined above and began advocating it as both the healthiest and most nutritionally fortifying start to the day.

At the time of Professor Schiøtz's work Oslo was an impoverished city, and the events of the First World War had further hampered its (and indeed the entire country's) ability to sustain its increasingly needy population. Malnourishment and dietary deficiencies, and the health conditions triggered by them, were rife. Schiøtz's breakfast provided an easy cure: its ingredients were cheap, nutritious, readily available, and – crucially – served cold, allaying any concerns over the cost of cooking or reheating. Understandably, given the state of the city at the time, his menu soon attracted attention.

Trials were held at schools in Oslo and Bergen to test the efficacy of Schiøtz's breakfast, and their results were staggering: pupils given Schiøtz's food rather than a stodgy midday meal gained weight, proved more resilient to infection, and exhibited both increased vitality and improved academic performance. By 1932, consequently, every schoolchild in Oslo was being served his recommended meal.

Word of Schiøtz's success soon spread, and before long the *Oslo breakfast* had gained worldwide attention. In Britain, America, Australia, and throughout the rest of Europe, its merits were tested, debated and eventually advocated everywhere from the daily presses to the highest levels of government. 'This Extra Meal Made Norwegian Children Grow 4 Inches!' declared America's *Life* magazine in 1943, reporting that those children who followed Schiøtz's diet routinely 'grew taller and huskier than others'. A trial in London in 1939 proved equally successful:

'The effects have been remarkable,' claimed one advocate, 'and have been particularly noticeable in the excellent complexions of the children and their freedom from the usual skin complaints of the town child.'

The scheme endured during the Second World War, albeit with a handful of amendments and regional variations: it's unlikely British schoolchildren would have been impressed when Professor Schiøtz later decided that one of those meagre slices of bread and margarine should be replaced with a hard-tack sandwich smeared with smoked herring. But by the later 1940s, rationing was beginning to take its toll, and by the early 1950s newfound tastes, fashions, post-war prosperity and better-equipped domestic kitchens all conspired against it. By the 1960s, the *Oslo breakfast* had all but fallen by the nutritional roadside, even in its native Norway.

Still, there's no denying the evidence and, as a fortifying breakfast, it probably can't go far wrong.

9

YTTERBY, SWEDEN

yttrium

Pity poor Norway. Its two contributions to our itinerary comprise *maelstrom*, a name no longer used on any maps, and the *Oslo breakfast*, a little-heard-of diet abandoned sixty years ago. To add salt to under-representation wounds, across the border in Sweden you'll find a tiny unassuming village, on an island barely a single square mile in size, that has contributed not just one but four different words to our language and has provided the scientific community with a whole lot more than that.

The village in question is Ytterby, which stands on the islet of Resarö in the Stockholm archipelago. To it we owe the words *yttrium*, *terbium*, *erbium* and *ytterbium* – the names of chemical elements numbers 39, 65, 68 and 70.

Several places around the globe have been immortalised on the periodic table,* two of which lie ahead of us on this trip. But considerably fewer places have been immortalised more than once: if you count both *californium* and *berkelium*, named after Berkeley National Laboratory, then California makes this

---

* Even Scotland has one in the form of *strontium*, which was discovered in rocks mined near the village of Strontian in the Scottish Highlands in 1790.

select list with two, while thanks to *germanium*, *darmstadtium* and *bassium*, Germany has three. But Ytterby appears in the etymologies of no fewer than four different elements. So how did such an insignificant spot come to have such unique scientific importance?

In the late eighteenth century a mine was opened on the outskirts of Ytterby to raid the rich deposits of quartz and feldspar found nearby. As demand for both minerals increased (quartz was used in the manufacture of iron, feldspar in the manufacture of porcelain), the mine was steadily expanded and deepened, eventually unearthing something considerably more exciting than feldspar.

In 1787, an amateur mineralogist named Carl Axel Arrhenius stumbled across a peculiarly dense black rock in a pile of rubble and other waste material from the Ytterby mine. Arrhenius wagered that the seemingly unique rock – which he named *ytterbite* – must contain a deposit of the newly discovered element tungsten, and so sent a sample to Johan Gadolin, professor of chemistry at the Finnish Royal Academy, for a second opinion.

After much experimentation, Gadolin concluded that far from containing mere tungsten, roughly a third of Arrhenius's extraordinary rock was comprised of an oxide of an entirely new, and as yet unidentified, chemical element.* What Gadolin didn't know, however, was that even that remarkable discovery was just the tip of a very significant scientific iceberg.

Gadolin could only describe the properties of his new discovery, as the techniques and equipment available to him at the time prevented him from isolating a pure sample. Instead, it fell to later chemists and their ever improving scientific knowhow

---

* For his work on ytterbite, the mineral was eventually renamed *gadolinite* in Johan Gadolin's honour.

to pick up where his work had left off. So, in 1797, the Swedish chemist Anders Gustaf Ekeberg confirmed Gadolin's findings, and named the oxide he had discovered *yttria*, in honour of Arrhenius's *ytterbite*. In 1828, a sample of the element Gadolin had predicted was finally isolated by the German chemist Friedrich Wöhler, who named it *yttrium*. Next to pick up the case was a Swedish chemist named Carl Gustaf Mosander, who in 1843 found that Ekeberg's *yttria* was actually a mixture of three different oxides, which he named *yttria*, *terbia* and *erbia*; terbia and erbia, he later discovered, each contained their own unique chemical elements too, which he gave the names *terbium* and *erbium*. Finally, in 1878, the Swiss chemist Jean-Charles de Marignac separated one final element from Gadolin's sample, which he gave the name *ytterbium*.*

All four of these elements – *yttrium*, *terbium*, *erbium* and *ytterbium* – were given names honouring the tiny mining town where their source mineral had been found, entirely by chance, almost a century earlier. Ytterby's unique place in the scientific canon was ultimately assured – but, even then, Arrhenius's ytterbite still had a few secrets left to reveal.

By the end of the nineteenth century, samples of Arrhenius's rock were being analysed and investigated independently by scientists all across Europe. The discoveries kept on coming. In 1878, a Swedish chemist and biologist named Per Teodor Cleve found two further elements in a sample of the oxide erbia, which he named *holmium* (after the Latin name for Stockholm, *Holmia*) and *thulium* (after *Thule*, a classical name for Scandinavia). In 1879, fellow Swedish chemist Lars Fredrik Nilson discovered another new element, which he named *scandium* in honour of its native Scandinavia. In 1886, French chemist Paul-Émile Lecoq

---

* In 1880, de Marignac discovered another new element, which he named *gadolinium* in Johan Gadolin's honour.

de Boisbaudran* isolated another element from erbium ores, which he gave a name, *dysprosium*, quite appropriately derived from the Greek for 'hard to obtain'. And lastly, one final element was discovered in a sample of Arrhenius's rock in 1907, which the French scientist Georges Urbain named *lutetium*, in honour of the Roman name for Paris, *Lutetia*.

Had the architects of these final few discoveries had a few more letters left to play with in the name *Ytterby*, it's tempting to presume that the town's contribution to the periodic table might have been even greater. But there's only so much you can do with a seven-letter word, so they had to look elsewhere for their etymological inspiration. Nevertheless, all in all that peculiar black rock found on the rubbish heap of a feldspar mine outside the tiny village of Ytterby had given the world eight new rare earth metals and the dictionary four extraordinary new words.

---

* Another of Paul-Émile Lecoq de Boisbaudran's discoveries was the chemical element *gallium*, which he found via spectroscopy in 1875. He named his discovery in honour of his native France, the Latin name for which was *Gallia*, but rumours soon emerged that de Boisbaudran had also cheekily intended to name his discovery after himself: *Le coq* is French for 'rooster', which in Latin is *gallus*. Convention at the time preferred scientists to avoid such self-aggrandising practices, and de Boisbaudran came under so much criticism that he felt compelled to deny the suggestion and reiterate the name's true origin in a paper published in 1877. 'On August 27, 1875,' he wrote, 'between three and four at night, I perceived the first indications of the existence of a new element that I named gallium in honor of France, *Gallia*.'

10

Helsinki, Finland

Finlandisation

F rom Sweden, we cross both the border and the Baltic, and head for Finland.

Admittedly, besides the word *sauna*, the Finnish language hasn't contributed an awful lot to English. In fact if you were to compile a list of Finlandisms we English speakers have borrowed over the centuries, you would have to resort to plundering the dictionary for obscure gems such as *rapakivi* (a type of granite), *kantele* (a Finnish zither), *puukko* (a hook-shaped knife), and *rya* (a traditional Finnish knot-pile rug). Indeed until English finds the need to adopt eminently useful Finnish words like *peninkulma* ('the furthest distance at which a barking dog can still be heard'*) and *poronkusema* ('the distance a reindeer can walk without stopping to urinate'†), it's unlikely that list will grow any longer.

You can, however, thank Finnish speakers for naming the *Molotov cocktail* (if 'thank' is quite the right word to use here). During the Winter War of 1939, Soviet foreign minister

---

* Now sadly obsolete even in its native Finland, the *peninkula* was a unit of distance roughly reckoned to be around 3.3 miles . . .

† . . . and that's 4.6 miles, should you ever need to know.

Vyacheslav Molotov* fiercely (and dishonestly) denied that the Soviet Union was dropping incendiary bombs on their Finnish neighbours, and instead claimed that they were dropping food parcels to help starving Finns through the harsh winter. The ever resourceful and sardonic Finns in return nicknamed these bombs *Molotov bread-baskets* and, requiring a little something to wash them down with, labelled the impromptu fuel-filled incendiaries they used to attack Soviet tanks *Molotov cocktails*.

Finland's prickly relationship with its neighbour to the east is also the origin of the word that brings us here: *Finlandisation*. Unfortunately, it's yet another word coined in the heat of war – only the war that led to this particular term was cold.

Finland shares eight hundred miles of its eastern border with Russia, and as a result the two nations have endured a long and often uneasy history. In 1809, Finland was incorporated into the Russian empire, but after the Russian Revolution in 1917 it declared its independence and has remained independent ever since.

During the Second World War, however, Russia repeatedly attempted to occupy and regain its former Finnish territories; the Finns retaliated strongly, and in all only one-tenth of the country changed hands during the war. When hostilities finally ceased and the United Nations was formed in 1945, Finland officially adopted a policy of neutrality, but during the Cold War that followed, it once again found itself in a precarious situation.

In 1948, with an increasingly formidable and ever more belligerent superpower just across the border, Finland was compelled to sign an official Agreement of Friendship, Cooperation and Mutual Assistance with the Soviet Union. The treaty obliged

---

* Molotov's real name was Vjačeslav Mihajlovič Skrjabin. His alias, *Molotov*, was derived from the Russian word for 'hammer', *molot* – just as Joseph Stalin (Iosif Vissarionovich Dzhugashvili) took a pseudonym derived from the Russian for 'steel', *stal*, and Vladimir Lenin (Vladimir Ilyich Ulyanov) earned a nickname apparently honouring Russia's River Lena.

Finland to resist any Western invasion of Soviet territory via Finnish territory, even if that meant calling on the Soviet military assistance to do so. In signing the agreement, the Finns also had to accept some Soviet influence on their politics, but crucially it allowed Finland to remain independent in the shadow of its undoubtedly imposing neighbour, and saw off the growing threat of a Soviet invasion.

As the Cold War deepened and East–West relations became even frostier, the West increasingly saw Finland's uneasy relationship with Russia as an unwelcome appeasement and a quiet tolerance of the Soviet Union's growing belligerence – and it was this that became known as *Finlandisation*. As the *Oxford English Dictionary* explains it, the term refers to the state of being compelled 'to favour, or refrain from opposing, the interests of the former Soviet Union despite not being formally allied to it politically'.

Precisely who coined the term is unclear. Austrian foreign minister Karl Gruber is one of those often credited with its invention; he reportedly warned his country not to follow the Finns' example as early as 1953. But the earliest record of the word *Finlandisation* itself (or rather its German equivalent, *Finnlandisierung*) is credited to German political scientist Richard Löwenthal, who in 1961 theorised that it was the Finlandisation, not Communisation, of vulnerable European nations that was the Soviet Union's ultimate Cold War goal.

Whatever its origins, the term remained in vogue in political discourse throughout the 1960s and 1970s, but when the Soviet Union collapsed in the early 1990s (and Finland tore up its agreement in 1992), *Finlandisation* began to fall out of use.

It survives today in a more generalised sense, referring to any country that finds itself obliged, for whatever reason, to tolerate or remain neutral towards a larger or more formidable neighbour that exercises considerable influence over it. The word's actual association with Finland may be a thing of the past but *Finlandisation* itself, alas, lives on.

11

DUBNA, RUSSIA

dubnium

inlandisation may be behind us (in more ways than one) but Russia now lies ahead of us – as does one more visit to the chemistry lab.

Russia is namechecked in a number of English words and phrases, from *Russian law* (a seventeenth-century expression for especially severe justice*) to the vodka-heavy *black Russian* cocktail (which was actually invented in Belgium†). The name *Russia* itself was Victorian slang for a gentleman's pocketbook (so called as they were often made of Russian leather), while the game *Chinese whispers* or *telephone* – in which a whispered message is secretly relayed from player to player – started life back in the mid nineteenth century as *Russian scandal*:

---

* 'Let him have Russian law for all his sins,' reads a line in Thomas Dekker's 1623 play *The Wonder of a Kingdom*. '100 blowes on his bare shins.'

† The *Moscow mule* cocktail, likewise, is said to have been invented not in Moscow but in New York City by bartender Wes Price. According to an account published in the *Wall Street Journal* in 2007, Price mixed Smirnoff vodka with ginger beer for no reason other than that he 'wanted to clean out the basement', and rid his bar of a backlog of its worst-selling drinks.

46

There is a game called Russian Scandal, which is played in this fashion: A tells B a brief narrative, which B is to repeat to C, and C to D, and so on ... By the time the narrative has been transmitted from mouth to mouth six or seven times, it has commonly undergone a complete transformation. The ordinary result of the experiment will afford an apt illustration of the value of oral testimony.
—The London Quarterly Review (1861)

For obvious reasons, the expression *Russian scandal* also eventually came to be used figuratively of gossip or unreliable testimony.

What brings us to Russia now, however, is an actual Russian scandal – one that at the height of the Cold War led to yet another (although somewhat less threatening) disagreement between the East and West.

Twelve hundred miles ago we were in an unassuming Swedish mining town now immortalised in the periodic table. Arriving in Dubna – another equally unassuming town, some seventy-five miles north of Moscow – we've found another. Dubna gave its name to *dubnium*, a highly radioactive element with the atomic number 105.

Dubnium is a synthetic element, meaning it exists in no naturally occurring form, and so has to be artificially synthesised in laboratories. As a consequence, only a few atoms of it have ever been produced since its discovery in the late 1960s, and even the most stable of these have belonged to isotopes with a half-life of barely a single day. To say that science doesn't know an awful lot about dubnium is something of an understatement.

But while the physicists might have to sit this discussion out, the etymologists have plenty to talk about.

Dubnium is so named because its very first traces were supposedly produced by a team of scientists at the Soviet Joint Institute for Nuclear Research in Dubna in 1967. The same team finally confirmed their findings and successfully synthesised a sample of the element three years later. Around the same time, a team of scientists working at Berkeley National Laboratory at the University of California also claimed to have synthesised element 105, and likewise announced their discovery in early 1970. Precisely which team had got there first was unclear. That led to a problem.

By convention, the discoverers of new chemical elements earn the right to name their discovery themselves. But in the case of element 105, there were two separate teams staking independent claims – and each had its own idea of what it should be called. The Soviet team at Dubna wanted to call its discovery *nielsbohrium*, in honour of the acclaimed Danish physicist Niels Bohr. The Berkeley team championed the name *hanhium*, honouring the 'Father of Nuclear Chemistry', German scientist Otto Hahn. At the height of the Cold War, another East–West skirmish appeared to be on the cards. And just like the Cold War, this one was going to get worse before it got better.

In 1969, the Berkeley team announced to the scientific community that it had also successfully synthesised element 104, which they declared should now be named *rutherfordium*, in honour of the New Zealand-born physicist Ernest Rutherford. The problem was, however, that the Dubna team had again apparently got there first: the Soviets claimed that they had produced a sample of element 104 five years earlier, in 1964. Their means were unverified, but that didn't stop them coming up with their own suggestion for its name, *kurchatovium*, in honour of the director of the Soviet atomic-bomb project, Igor Kurchatov.

There were now two elements on the periodic table – numbers 104 and 105 – whose discoveries were both being independently claimed by Soviet and American research teams. Moreover, the Americans did not accept the Soviets' name or precedence, and vice versa.

Then, just to complicate things further, along came element 106.

In 1974, once again the team at Dubna announced that it had successfully synthesised another highly radioactive element, atomic number 106. Once again, just a few months later, the Berkeley team followed suit, and made precisely the same announcement.

This time, the US team made the first move and suggested the name *seaborgium* for their discovery, in honour of the American nuclear chemist Glenn T. Seaborg.* Helpfully, the Soviet team sat this one out, and made no suggestion of its own. (Perhaps it knew its claim was flawed, as in 1992 the method used by the Soviet team was finally found to be unsatisfactory.)

The naming disputes over these high-end chemical elements came to be known collectively as the 'Transfermium Wars', as they concerned all those elements listed above and beyond fermium, element number 100, on the periodic table. These 'wars' rumbled on for another two decades, despite the brokering of a series of compromises in the mid 1970s that saw all these contentious names being temporarily replaced with purely systematic ones: for a time, elements 104, 105 and 106 ultimately became known as *unnilquadium*, *unnilpentium* and *unnilhexium*, using neutral names based merely on the Latin for 1 (*un*), 0 (*nil*), 4 (*quad*), 5 (*pent*) and 6 (*hex*).

It wasn't until the late 1990s that the dispute was finally ended, when the International Union of Pure and Applied Chemistry approved the Berkeley team's suggested names for

---

* In fact, the US team had been trying to name an element *seaborgium* since the early 1950s: Seaborg was a pioneer in the field of synthesising elements, and when the possibility of manufacturing elements with atomic numbers above 99 was first announced, the suggestion was made that the first of these to be produced should be named in his honour. In fact, element 99 came to be named *einsteinium*.

elements 104, *rutherfordium*, and 106, *seaborgium*.* As for element 105, the IUPAC decided that it was to be named *dubnium*, in honour not of the original Soviet team's suggestion, but rather the team's work on the discovery. The so-called Transfermium Wars, ultimately, outlasted the Cold War they had so inadvertently mirrored.

* In approving the name *seaborgium*, the IUPAC was compelled to break its own moratorium on naming chemical elements after living scientists: when the name was finally approved in 1997, Glenn T. Seaborg was still alive. Seaborg later commented that this was 'the greatest honor ever bestowed upon me – even better, I think, than winning the Nobel Prize'. He died two years later, in 1999.

12

BALAKLAVA, UKRAINE

balaclava

A thousand miles to the south of Dubna lies the Crimean village of Balaklava.

Although today it might be more associated with crime than with Crimea, the *balaclava* helmet – a warm, usually woollen, item of headgear that covers most of the head, neck and face – famously takes its name from the strategically significant port of Balaklava on Ukraine's Black Sea coast. The garment itself has a long history: it originated in the thick, low hoods of cloaks worn as far back as the Middle Ages, which eventually became detachable and morphed into entirely separate items of headgear originally known as 'Templar' or 'uhlan' caps.

But if the *balaclava* as we know it already had a name, why rename it after a town in southern Ukraine? Well, to answer that we need to travel back to 25 October 1854, and one of the most infamous days in British military history.

By the winter of 1854, the Crimean War had already been raging for a year, and it would be another year and a half before the Treaty of Paris would bring hostilities to an end. Twelve months into the conflict came the Battle of Balaklava. An alliance of British, French and Ottoman troops clashed with the Russian empire, which was trying to take control of the port and thereby disrupt the allies' supply chain.

In the end, the allies successfully defended the port but lost control of one of their most important supply routes, which was ferrying much-needed food and equipment to the nearby besieged city of Sevastopol. The battle was therefore indecisive, but its impact would nevertheless be momentous.

By 9.30 on the morning of 25 October, the allies had already secured two significant victories. Under the command of Sir Colin Campbell, an infantry unit of the 93rd Highlanders had seen off two terrifying Russian cavalry charges, while Sir James Scarlett's Heavy Brigade – no more than three hundred cavalrymen – had routed some two thousand Russian troops in an extraordinary show of force that had taken just ten minutes. The allies ultimately seemed to be in the ascendancy, but as the Russian cavalry retreated over the hilltops and the Heavy Brigade began to celebrate victory, word reached the secondary Light Brigade that Lord Raglan, in overall command of the British forces, now wanted them to advance rapidly into the fray.

The order seemed absurd: in the aftermath of a victory that had already been secured, Raglan was apparently telling the Light Brigade to charge forward into a blind valley surrounded on three sides by scores of Russian troops. But the Brigade, under the command of Lord Cardigan, knew it had to obey no matter how suicidal the order seemed. As Alfred, Lord Tennyson would later put it, 'Theirs not to reason why, / Theirs but to do and die.'*

---

* Tennyson's 'The Charge of the Light Brigade' (1854) is one of his most popular and famous poems. Less well known is the poem he wrote nearly twenty years after the Crimean War celebrating the more successful

By the time the Charge of the Light Brigade was over – barely twenty minutes later – one sixth of the six hundred or more men who had entered the north valley of Balaklava had been killed. Nearly as many again had been injured or captured, and almost four hundred horses had been lost.

It later transpired that Lord Raglan's order had actually been for the Light Brigade merely to advance after the retreating Russian troops, to prevent them from capturing British guns that had been positioned in the surrounding hills. But as the order had been passed from messenger to messenger, it had become corrupted and truncated, so that by the time it reached Lord Cardigan, all that the Light Brigade was told to do was 'advance rapidly' back into the battle.

The blunder cost the allies dearly, and when news broke of the bloody Charge of the Light Brigade, it soon gained a reputation as one of the British Army's most disastrous missteps. Admittedly, some later historians have been more forgiving, suggesting that the insane bravery demonstrated by the British in charging into near certain death unnerved the Russian side. But there's little argument that this was an ignominious end to what could otherwise have been a decisive Allied victory.

That ignominy, however, had a curious linguistic consequence, as the battle left a lasting impression not just on English history, but on the English language. And we're not just talking about balaclava helmets.

According to reports, Lord Cardigan (like most British officers at the time) happened to be wearing a distinctive short, light, close-fitting woollen waistcoat on the day of the battle; the

'Charge of the Heavy Brigade' (1882) that had taken place earlier that morning:

> *The charge of the gallant three hundred, the Heavy Brigade!*
> *Down the hill, down the hill, thousands of Russians,*
> *Thousands of horsemen, drew to the valley – and stay'd . . .*

cardigan ultimately came to be named in his honour. Lord Raglan, meanwhile, was wearing a thick overcoat with noticeably wide, loose sleeves; it likewise came to be known as a *raglan* jacket.*
Sir Colin Campbell's red-coated Scottish troops had succeeded in seeing off those two early Russian cavalry charges by forming one long narrow line of men, standing two abreast; war reporters referred to it as a 'thin red line', a phrase that eventually became synonymous with any meagre yet fiercely effective defence. And, of course, the thick woollen helmets that the British troops had taken to wearing to protect themselves from the brutal weather of the Crimean mountains came to be known by the name of the battle at which they had been worn.

Curiously, the earliest written evidence we have of one of these helmets being called a *balaclava* dates from 1881, some twenty-five years after the Crimean War was over. Perhaps the fact that the battle's name had remained current until then is testimony to how significant, and infamous, the event had been.

* Lord Raglan had lost an arm at the Battle of Waterloo in 1815, and preferred this distinctive type of jacket as it disguised his missing limb: the sleeve fabric was looser and extended all the way to the neckline rather than stopping at the shoulder, a style that is now known as a *raglan* sleeve.

13

ISTANBUL, TURKEY

turkey

From Crimea we cross the Black Sea to Turkey, a country that has plenty to keep the etymological traveller busy.

Angora wool, for instance, and the *angora* goats from which it comes, both take their name from the Turkish capital of Ankara, which was known as Angora until 1930.* The word *solecism* comes from the Ancient Greek city of Soloi, near modern-day Mezitli on Turkey's south coast, whose populace reportedly spoke such a crude dialect that the city's name eventually morphed into a term for any sentence that breaks the rules of grammar. And the name of ancient Phrygian city of Laodicea, near modern-day Denizli, is the origin of the criminally underused adjective *laodicean*, meaning 'apathetic' or 'lukewarm'; the word namechecks the ancient Laodicean Church, one of the seven so-called Churches of the Revelation singled out in the Bible and attacked for its religious indifference:

---

* *Angora* cats and rabbits, meanwhile, are so called because their long silky fur resembles the goats' soft wool.

*And unto the angel of the church of the Laodiceans write . . . I
know thy works, that thou art neither cold nor hot: I would thou
wert cold or hot. So then, because thou art lukewarm and neither
cold nor hot, I will spue thee out of my mouth.*
—Revelation (3:14–16)

The intricate architecture (and equally intricate political machi-
nations) of Byzantium, the ancient name of Istanbul, is the origin
of our word *Byzantine*, referring to anything impossibly complex
or convoluted. According to etymological legend, the equally
ancient city of Chalcedon (now Kadıköy, a suburb of Istanbul)
has its name immortalised in that of the precious stone *chalcedony*.
At the entrance to the Bosporus strait at Istanbul are a group of
small rocky outcrops known in ancient times as the Symplegades.
Legend has it that these rocks would clash together and destroy
any vessel that dared sail past them, and so their name has
become a metaphor for any dangerous or precarious situation.

Despite all of these stories, however, what brings us to
Turkey now is perhaps one of the most obvious (and yet one of
the most complicated) linguistic stories the country has to offer.
So the burning question is, why are turkeys called *turkeys*?

According to the *Oxford English Dictionary*, the earliest reference to a turkey we know about in English dates from 1541,
when a 'turkeycocke' was listed as one of several 'greater fyshes
or fowles' available on the menu to Tudor diners. This probably
wasn't the same turkey we have at Christmas and Thanksgiving:
back in the mid sixteenth century, the birds we now know as
turkeys had yet to make much of an impact on European cuisine,
and so this Tudor-period *turkey* was probably an African guinea
fowl, a pheasant, or even a peacock. (Or, perhaps more likely, the
word was merely intended to be a catch-all term for any exotic-
looking bird imported onto Europe dining tables via traders in
the eastern Mediterranean.)

It wasn't until later in the sixteenth century that turkeys as we know them today began to be imported in any considerable number across the Atlantic from Europe's colonies in their native North America. As just another plump, peculiar-looking bird that roasted well and came from some far-flung land, it too came under the catch-all heading all other similar birds had: the *turkey*, both in name and form, had finally arrived – from the opposite direction from its namesake country.

Over time, this American turkey steadily grew in popularity, and the name *turkey* became all but exclusively attached to it, falling out of use as a byword for any exotic fowl and leaving us with the bird, and indeed the word, as it is today.

Happily, the English language isn't alone in its geographical struggle with the humble turkey. In French, for instance, the turkey is known as *le coq d'inde*, or simply *dinde* – a name that refers directly (and equally mistakenly) to India. Speakers of Polish (*indyk*), Basque (*indioliar*) and Armenian (who know the turkey as the *hndikahav*, or 'Indian chicken') all make the same error.

Things get even more specific in the likes of Dutch (*kalkoen*), Swedish (*kalkon*), and Norwegian (*kalkun*), all of which name-check the Indian trade port of Calicut in their words for 'turkey'. In Portugal, things are even more confused: the Portuguese for 'turkey' is *peru*, which mistakenly refers to the South American country conquered by the Spanish at around the same time turkeys began to appear on European tables.

With most European languages apparently suffering some kind of turkey-related geographical misstep, it's worth mentioning that those ever astute Luxembourgers dodge the issue altogether and implement a much more pragmatic solution. Rather than referencing the turkey's supposed country of origin, Luxembourgish speakers allude instead to its striking nasal wattles in their word, *Schnuddelhong* – which literally means 'snot-hen'.

And on that note, it's time to move on . . . Soon, we'll be heading to Greece, but before that, let's take a brief tour of some Mediterranean islands.

14

NICOSIA, CYPRUS

copper

S ome etymologists believe the humble *sardine* takes its name from the Italian island of Sardinia. The Ancient Greeks knew Sardinia as *Sardo*, and it's possible that the fish were once caught in such impressive numbers off the Sardinian coast that the island gave the fish their Greek name, *sardinos*. It's just a theory, however, and a fairly fishy one at that: it's questionable whether or not the Greeks would have had the maritime capabilities to catch fish as far afield as Sardinia at around the time the word first appeared in print in the fourth century BCE.

The Greeks certainly knew about Sardinia, however, as they have given us the word *sardonic*, meaning 'sarcastic' or 'false'. To the Greeks, *sardonic* laughter was known as *sardonios gelos*, or literally 'Sardinian laughter'; the Greeks believed that eating a toxic Sardinian plant known as *sardonion* caused people to make grotesque facial convulsions that looked like mocking laughter before they died. And that's no joke.

But Sardinia isn't the only Mediterranean island namechecked in the dictionary. *Majolica* pottery takes its name from the island of Majorca, while the island's capital, Mahon, provides one of a number of possible explanations for the origin of *mayonnaise*. A *mellinder* is a beautifully named seventeenth-century sweet pastry, thought to conflate the Latin words for 'honey', *mel*, and 'Malta', *Melita* (via an Old French word, *melite*, that meant 'promised land' or 'land of plenty').

Something that is *hyblaean* is equally honeyed or mellifluous, an allusion to the fine-quality honey made in the hills around the ancient city of Hybla, on Sicily. *Marsala* wine takes its name from the Sicilian seaport of Marsala, from where it was first exported to England in any great quantity in the eighteenth century. And off the coast of Sicily is a vast whirlpool, known in ancient times as Charybdis. Paired up with the name of a sea monster, Scylla, said to dwell in the nearby Straits of Messina, *to be between Scylla and Charybdis* is to be in a position where one has to choose between two equally unpleasant alternatives.*

Cyprus, at the far eastern end of the Mediterranean, six hundred miles south of Istanbul, has a long history, much inter-twined with that of nearby Greece and Asia Minor. The Cypriot city of Paphos on the island's southwest coast, for instance, is said to have been the birthplace of Aphrodite, the Greek goddess of love, beauty and procreation, and it's from there that the English language picked up the sixteenth-century adjective *paphian*, meaning 'sexual' or 'desirous'. A *paphian shot* is one of Cupid's arrows. The noun *paphian* is a fairly subtle euphemism for a prostitute.

But Cyprus has a lot more to offer the dictionary than just words to do with love, romance and, er, prostitution.

To the Romans, Cyprus was well known for its copper mines, and the metal obtained from these mines became known as

---

* In Homer's *Odyssey*, Odysseus is forced to sail the straits between Scylla and Charybdis; he opts to pass more closely by Scylla, and risk losing only one or two sailors to the monster, rather than risk the entire ship to Charybdis.

aes cyprium, or the 'metal of Cyprus'.* The Latin *cyprium* morphed over time into *cuprum*, and it's from there that the English language eventually picked up the word *copper* sometime around the early eleventh century.† So not only do we owe one of our most everyday of words to Cyprus, but there's a good chance you can thank the island for the contents of your back pocket, or what you might find hidden down the back of your sofa.

* While *cyprium* eventually morphed into *copper*, the Latin word *aes* eventually inspired our word *ore*. Ironically, just as we consider copper coins to be loose change or cash, the Latin word *aes* could also be used to mean 'money' or 'cash'.

† The Latin *cuprum* is also the origin of the somewhat counter-intuitive chemical symbol for copper, Cu.

15

ABDERA, GREECE

Abderian laughter

From Cyprus, we head back to the European mainland for a quick sight-seeing tour of Greece – a destination that perhaps has more to offer us than any other.

The number of Greek – or, as is more often the case, Ancient Greek – locations that crop up in the etymologies of words in the dictionary is remarkable. Some of these are staggeringly familiar. *Chestnuts*, for instance, are literally 'Castanean nuts', perhaps first cultivated in the town of Castana in Thessaly, while *currants* take their name from the fact that they were sold in Britain originally as 'raisins of Corinth' in the fourteenth century.

If you've ever described something as *spartan*, or someone as *laconic*, then you've namechecked the Ancient Greek city state of Sparta (whose people were known for their frugality and bravery) and its surrounding region of Laconia (whose populace were reportedly known for their terse 'laconic' speech).

The Olympic *marathon* famously takes its name from the battle fought between the Greeks and Persians at Marathon in 490 BCE – while its 26.2-mile length is supposedly the distance the messenger Pheidippides had to run to bring news of the Greeks' victory to Athens. Marathon itself was a city in Ancient Attica, the region of central Greece from which we have taken the word *attic*: classical Attic architecture was characterised by small decorative columns or walls above the main facades of buildings, but eventually the word came to refer to any space enclosed by the walls above the main structure of a building, and ultimately the space enclosed by its roof.

At the less familiar end of this Ancient Greek scale are a host of ever more obscure words such as *lacedemonian*, a synonym for 'spartan' derived from the province of Lacedaemon in Laconia, and *boeotian*, a sixteenth-century adjective meaning 'stupid' or 'dull', in allusion to the proverbial stupidity of the people of Boeotia in central Greece. *Actium*, the name of a town and promontory on Greece's west coast, can be used as a byword for any decisive, crushing defeat, as it was here that the Roman Empire trounced Marc Antony and Cleopatra in a fierce naval battle in 31 BCE.

The name of another famous Greek battle, *Thermopylae*, has become a popular reference to any heroic, last-ditch defence or attempt to rout an opposing force. The name of a narrow pass in rural Thessaly, it was at Thermopylae that a force of three hundred Spartans famously stood off the entire Persian Army in 480 BCE.

Something described as *Arcadian* is ideally and idyllically rural, or utterly peaceful and utopian, a reference to the peaceful mountainous region of Arcadia in central Greece. The adjectives *Parnassian*, *Pierian* and *Heliconian* can all be used to mean 'poetic' or 'artistic', a reference to the Muses of Greek legend supposedly living atop Mount Parnassus in Pieria, a region of northern Greece, and holding the springs on Mount Helicon in sacred regard. The name of Mount Pelion in Thessaly can be used as a byword for any challenging or insurmountable difficulty; when paired up with nearby Mount Ossa, the expression *to pile Pelion upon Ossa* is to make the great even greater – or to make the already difficult even more difficult.

Elsewhere in Greece, in the far northeast corner, lies the long-ruined Thracian city of Abdera. Among its most noted citizens was a fifth-century-BCE philosopher and mathematician named Democritus. Given that he's believed to have lived well into his nineties (if not past a hundred), we can presume that he had quite the legacy to leave behind, but sadly, only the odd fragment of Democritus's life's work remains. Nevertheless, from stories and anecdotes retold and referenced long after his death, we know that a great deal of Democritus's philosophical writings were focused on the value of cheerfulness and optimism, and in his teaching he stressed the importance of always looking on the comic side of life.

Unfortunately, that particular world view has its drawbacks, and it's safe to say that it didn't go down too well with Democritus's more stoic contemporaries, among whom he soon gained a reputation for laughing incessantly, inanely, or entirely out of context. That reputation was ultimately passed on to all of Democritus's followers, and then to his fellow citizens of Abdera, so that eventually the adjective *Abderian* came to mean 'foolish', 'vacuous', or 'empty-headed'. *Abderian laughter* is the laughter of someone who will laugh at anything:

> *For my own part, I always tremble when I hear a story beginning 'What d'ye think?' – 'I'll tell you what,' – and such like useless exordiums. These are certain indications of a very empty head . . . There are some of the Insipids who, being a very merry set of empty animals, instead of using these articulate expletives, supply the place of sense with Abderian laughter; performing at once the equally disagreeable parts of troublesome, impertinent orators, and noisy auditors, bestowing upon themselves the applause which their insensible hearers omit giving them.*
> *—Memoirs of the Society of Grub-street, vol. 1 (1731)*

With a smile on our faces, we cross the Greek border to the north, heading into the fourth of the four Black Sea nations on our list.

16

SOFIA,
BULGARIA

buggery

It is becoming apparent that while some countries, like France and Greece, provide us with an embarrassment of linguistic riches, others have only a handful of etymological tales to tell. Bulgaria has seemingly afforded our language only one word out of the entire dictionary. The word in question is *buggery*.

Admittedly, to say that's the *only* English word Bulgaria is etymologically responsible for is a little unfair. There is an old theory that *buckram* fabric takes its name from a mangled corruption of Bulgaria's name. But that theory is fairly shaky,* and the linguistic evidence to back it up is admittedly lacking. So, for want of a better expression, that leaves us with *buggery*.

For any Bulgarians reading this, if it helps to remove some of the sting in this particular tail (so to speak), the word *buggery* hasn't always meant, well, 'buggery'. Back when it first appeared in the English language in the fourteenth century, *bugger* actually meant 'heretic', while *buggery* was merely a word for the most

---

* The more likely origin of *buckram* lies almost 2,500 miles away in what is now Uzbekistan – but more on that later . . .

heinous or disreputable form of religious dissent. So when the English chronicler Robert Mannyng wrote in the 1330s that '*the kyng said and did crie the Pope was heretike . . . and lyved in bugerie*', he didn't mean, well, 'buggery'.

Etymologically, *bugger* developed from its Norman French equivalent *bougre*, which in turn comes from the Latin word *Bulgarus*, literally meaning 'Bulgarian'. So how exactly did a word meaning 'Bulgarian' come to mean 'religious heretic'? And, for that matter, 'bugger'? Oddly, the missing link here is the name of an obscure religious sect, which swept across Europe in the late Middle Ages.

Founded by and named after a Bulgarian priest named Bogomil, Bogomilism was a radical religious movement that emerged in the Bulgarian empire sometime in the mid tenth century. The Bogomils, as its followers were known, spurned the sanctity of baptism and the Eucharist, rejected building churches and praying to crosses, and sought to reform and rebuild the newly established Bulgarian Orthodox Church.

The controversial movement proved popular, and spread quickly across southeast Europe, but that brought it into direct conflict with the Catholic Church. The Vatican dispatched missionaries to the Balkans in an attempt to hold this sweeping tide of Bogomilism at bay, but still it spread, steadily incorporating and allying itself with other radical sects and cults that popped up all across Europe at the time. To the Catholics, who were now facing a crisis on the eastern fringes of their influence, these dangerous religious upstarts all became disdainfully known by one single name, inspired by the Bogomils' geographical origins: together, these troublesome heretics were the 'Bulgarians'.

Because their teachings went against all those of the established Church (and perhaps partly in a propagandising attempt to whip up public hysteria against them), all manner of questionable practices soon began to be ascribed to these Bulgarians, regardless of whether they actually committed them or not.

Among the charges laid at their collective door were sodomy, homosexuality and even bestiality; heresy and doctrinal sin had finally become conflated with sexual sin. Because of a handful of historical and etymological missteps, the Bulgarians had finally become conflated with all the Catholic Church's most heinous notions of sexual depravity.

Thankfully for Bulgaria, as the Church's term-of-choice *Bulgarian* drifted from Latin into French and then English, its connection to its geographical meaning became obscured. The earliest reference to the crime of *buggery* in English law comes from a 1533 Act of Parliament, passed under Henry VIII, which outlaws and establishes punishments for the 'vice of buggerie' – by which time any obvious similarity to the name *Bulgaria* had clearly become watered down. Ultimately, the story of how one of Eastern Europe's proudest, most resilient and most pictur-esque countries came to be associated with sexual misconduct has long since been relegated to the etymological footnotes.

17

SKOPJE, MACEDONIA

macédoine

Leaving Bulgaria behind, we head west through Mediterranean Europe. Our first stop is Macedonia, the ancient nation sandwiched both culturally and geographically between Bulgaria, Greece, Albania and two fellow former Yugoslav republics, Serbia and Kosovo.

Like Bulgaria before it, the Macedonian contribution to our language isn't as robust as it is elsewhere. However, there is at least one word here that's worth stopping to admire:

> *Macédoine is a French word of modern coinage . . . It means a mixture of different fruits iced, such as confectioners prepare for desserts; also a round game at cards, when each player chooses his own in succession.*
> —Henry Luttrell, *Letters to Julia*, Third Edition (1822)

Literally speaking, the word *macédoine* is nothing more than the French name for Macedonia – so essentially we have here a word that means 'a fruit salad', 'a card game', and 'a former Yugoslav republic'. There can't be many of those in the dictionary surely. So where did it come from? And why, of all places, should it be Macedonia?

As the name of a medley of fruits, *macédoine* first appeared in its native French in the mid eighteenth century, before falling into use in English in the early 1800s. Its exotic-sounding name soon caught on with Victorian diners, and before long *macédoines* of everything from frozen fruits to glazed vegetables* were appearing in the menus and cookbooks of nineteenth-century England.

As for the card game, *macédoine* seemingly never much caught on in England, and has long since fallen out of fashion in its native France. As a result, precisely how it was played and what its rules entailed remain something of a mystery – but we do know a little something about it, thanks to a footnote to one of the greatest of all French novels:

> *Some readers may not know that a macédoine is a medley of several games of chance, among which each player has the right to choose when it is his turn to deal. It is one of the novelties of our day.*
> —Choderlos de Laclos, *Les Liaisons dangereuses* (1782)

The connection between Henry Luttrell's fruity mélange and the somewhat perplexing card game mentioned in *Dangerous Liaisons* is that they're both medleys of some description. What does that have to do with Macedonia? In truth, no one is entirely sure. But the popular theory concerns one of the most famous characters in all history.

Alexander the Great was born in Pella – now in the modern-day Greek region of Macedonia, not its Yugoslav neighbour to its north – in 356 BCE. He reigned over the kingdom of Macedonia for thirteen years, from the death of his father Philip II in 336 BCE

---

* According to Charles Elmé Francatelli's *The Modern Cook* (1846), a vegetable *macédoine* was made by mixing together diced cucumber, boiled peas, cauliflower florets, asparagus heads, French beans 'cut into the shape of diamonds', and 'some carrots and turnips in fancy shapes'.

to his own death in Babylon in 323 BCE, at the age of thirty-two. In that short time, Alexander extended the range of the Macedonian kingdom so greatly that by the time of his death it stretched from Greece and the Balkans in the west to the Nile valley in the south, and as far east as the Indian Ocean and the Himalayas. Some of the greatest cities in antiquity fell under his control – Ephesus, Jerusalem, Persepolis and Tyre among them – and Alexander ruled over Greeks, Persians, Phoenicians, Judaeans, Babylonians, Egyptians and Mesopotamians. In modern terms, his empire would have covered some twenty-two countries, from Serbia, Cyprus, Turkey and Egypt to Afghanistan, Tajikistan, Pakistan and India.

Few figures in history have ever wielded such power, let alone done so single-handedly – or, for that matter, by the age of thirty-two. But of all Alexander's achievements, what concerns us here is that impressive geographical inventory of peoples and nations over whom he once ruled. It is that that lies behind the *macédoine*: etymologically, what better name could there be for a medley of any kind than one that alludes to an empire, and an emperor, that once ruled over so diverse a group of peoples, and so many countries?

18

SARAJEVO, BOSNIA AND HERZEGOVINA

Balkanisation

From Macedonia we head northwest, passing through Albania, Kosovo, Serbia, and Montenegro, entering Bosnia and Herzegovina, the third-largest and centre-most of Europe's seven former Yugoslav republics.

We're right in the heart of the Balkan peninsula, a region that has given our language everything from *cravats* to *Dalmatians* (more on those in a moment). But here is also home to a word to which all the Balkan nations together can stake an etymological claim. Which is somewhat ironic, given what it means.

Balkanisation is the process by which a country or region fragments into a number of smaller constituent nations. In political contexts, the term is often used somewhat critically or disparagingly, to imply that these smaller constituent units remain mutually hostile or uncooperative, even after independence. The word has more recently gained a looser, more figurative sense, to mean merely 'to divide' or 'split'.

It's tempting to think that *Balkanisation* must be a relatively modern invention, referring to what feels like a relatively modern phenomenon. After all, it was only as recently as 1991 that the former Republic of Yugoslavia began to break up into the beguiling patchwork of nations that comprise the Balkan peninsula today. But so extraordinary is the Balkan region's history that the term actually dates back to the early twentieth century. 'How long the present Balkanisation of Europe is to continue,' announced Edward H. Bradford, dean of Harvard Medical School, in an address to the American College of Surgeons, 'and how much chaos is to result no one can tell.' Incredibly, Bradford delivered his address on 16 November 1914.

So what was occurring at that time to make Bradford's *balkanisation* worth mentioning?

By the second half of the 1800s, much of the Balkan peninsula was under the control of either the Austro-Hungarian or Ottoman Empire. As these two great superpowers began to crumble towards the end of the century, the swathe of nations and peoples over which they had dominion began to grow ever more restless. Before long, Greece, Serbia, Montenegro, Romania, Bulgaria and Albania had all gained some level of independence or autonomy, and the events of the First World War served only to complicate things further. Both great empires collapsed after the war, leading to the formation of several more new nations: Turkey, and an independent Austria and Hungary among them, as well as a newly united Kingdom of Yugoslavia.

It was against this backdrop of international tension and fragmentation that the word *balkanisation* was first coined in the early 1900s. But, as we now know, the process was by no means over.

Yugoslavia endured as a kingdom until war again broke out in 1939. Invaded and partitioned by the Axis powers during the Second World War, Yugoslavia became a republic in 1944. But the country struggled to maintain unity in the tumultuous decades that followed, until finally, in the early 1990s, Slovenia, Croatia and Macedonia all announced their independence; what remained of the former Yugoslav Republic collapsed the following year.

Since then, the process has continued: Serbia and Montenegro, initially united as a single federation in 1992, went their separate ways in 2006. And, although currently only partially recognised on the international stage, the Republic of Kosovo, barely half the size of Wales, declared its independence from Serbia two years later. Whether this process will continue in the twenty-first century remains to be seen.

We're not quite finished with the Balkans. When England reached the semi-finals of the football World Cup in 2018, it marked the first time the team had reached such an advanced stage for twenty-eight years. The achievement sparked an online meme listing several seemingly ubiquitous things that simply did not exist back in 1990: Facebook, Amazon, eBay, and YouTube all made the list, as did iPhones, iPods, Wikipedia and Google. One thing the list failed to mention, however, was England's opponent, Croatia. Twenty-eight years earlier it was still one of the constituent nations of Yugoslavia, and was yet to *balkanise* its way into independence. The last time England had reached the semi-finals, the Republic of Croatia simply did not exist.

19

ZAGREB, CROATIA

cravat

Croatia has a lot more to offer than viral memes and World Cup defeats. Without Croatia, there'd be no *101 Dalmatians*: the breed takes its name from Croatia's Dalmatian coastline, the narrowing belt of land along the Adriatic coast where the dogs were first bred in the seventeenth century. Without Croatia, there'd be no *argosy* ships: these merchant vessels, so large that their name became a byword for an entire fleet of ships, take their name from *Ragusa*, the Latin name for Dubrovnik. And without Croatia, the foppish dandies of the eighteenth and nineteenth centuries would not have been correctly attired:

> *DANDY was first applied half in admiration half in derision to a fop about the year 1816. [Early slang lexicographer] John Bee . . . gives as their peculiarities, 'French gait, lispings, wrinkled foreheads, killing king's English, wearing immense plaited pantaloons, coat cut away, small waistcoat, cravat and chitterlings immense, hat small, hair frizzled and protruding.'*
> —John S. Farmer and W. E. Henley, *Slang and Its Analogues Past and Present* (vol. 2, 1891)

No, it's not their 'plaited pantaloons' that these dandies can thank Croatia for: *pantaloons* take their name from *Pantalone*, a stock character in Italian Renaissance comedy, who typically wore a pair of ridiculously tight trousers.* Nor is it the dandies' immense 'chitterlings' that are Croatian; more familiar now as the name of a type of sausage, but back in the late 1500s a *chitterling* was an ornate type of neck ruff, so called because its frilled edge looked like the folds of a slaughtered animal's entrails. (No, really.)

In fact, it's the humble *cravat* that we owe to Croatia – although its association with the foppish dandies of the eighteenth century, like those described above, might be about as far removed from its fierce, soldierly origins as it's possible to go.

Cravat literally means 'Croat', and the word has its roots in the Croatian name for 'Croatia', *Hrvatska*. It was borrowed into English from French in the mid seventeenth century, but the garment to which it refers dates back to the late 1500s at least – around the time that bands of fierce mercenary cavalrymen from Eastern Europe were being drafted into the armies and conflicts of Central Europe.

At the time, much of the continent was embroiled in what would eventually become known as the Thirty Years War: a series of bloody religious conflicts fought from 1618 to 1648, between the constituent states of the Holy Roman Empire and several neighbouring and intervening foreign powers. To bolster their strength, many of the forces involved recruited mercenaries from the east, including Cossacks and Tatars from Russia and

* In these early *commedia dell'arte* comedies, Pantalone was meant to be a stereotypical caricature of a Venetian merchant: a wizened, money-grubbing old man, prowling the streets of one of Italy's most important trade ports looking for any opportunity to make money. Although there are a number of etymological theories behind his name, it's likely that *Pantalone* derives from St Pantaleon, one of the most important religious figures in Venetian culture (and the patron saint of lottery winners).

Ukraine, as well as fighters from Yugoslavia, Hungary, Poland and Romania. But it was under just one geographical name that this entire motley bunch came to be known to much of Europe: they were the *Croats* – and they were known for a little something else besides their military prowess.

Many of these Croat mercenaries wore a long linen neck scarf, tied or knotted loosely at the collar, which protected the neck and chest from the elements without restricting movement in battle. As the conflicts of the early 1600s rumbled on and more and more Croat troops began to be seen in the West, this style of neckband steadily grew in popularity, becoming less of a military necessity and more a chic fashion accessory. The ever stylish Parisians were probably the first to see the scarf's sartorial potential, and it's from France that the style caught on elsewhere; according to legend, it was Charles II and his supporters who brought this new style of scarf to England on his return from exile in the mid 1600s. Whatever its origins, however, before long the flamboyant pleated ruffs of the sixteenth century had become a thing of the past, replaced by these lighter, looser and lower-maintenance scarves and neckbands. The Croats' *cravat* had finally arrived.

Oddly, despite its origins among fierce mercenaries, the cravat was initially a unisex garment, but by the late eighteenth century all that had changed: as ever more colours, patterns, fabrics and styles of knot became available, the cravat became an ever more foppish accessory, and soon established itself as the pre-eminent gentleman's fashion statement of the day.

An anonymous pamphlet of 1818 outlined as many as fourteen different ways of tying one's cravat, from 'The Mathematical' ('so-called from its triangular form') to 'The Oriental' (best made with a 'very stiff and rigid cloth', apparently) and 'The Ballroom' ('quite delicious' when worn well). As any self-respecting cravat wearer knows, of course, one should always avoid the 'Horse Collar' look:

The Horse Collar has become, from some unaccountable reason,
very universal. I can only attribute it to the inability of its wear-
ers to make any other. It is certainly the worst and most vulgar,
and I should not have given it a place in these pages were it not
for the purpose of cautioning my readers, from ever wearing it.
— *The Neckclothitania, or Tietania* (1818)

The cravat fell into and out of fashion over the decades that
followed, virtually disappearing towards the end of the nineteenth century before seeing a revival in the 1960s and 1970s.
Regardless of its popularity, however, the word itself at least has
remained current throughout.

20

KÓCS, HUNGARY

coach

We now pause in three tiny towns, each hidden away in Central Europe, and each having made an indelible contribution to the English language. In the case of at least two of the next few stops on our journey, the words in question are in constant use.

Kócs (pronounced *kotch*) is a village in northwest Hungary, some forty miles from Budapest, home to only a little over two thousand people. From this small village, however, comes a word that can be used to mean any one of a number of modes of transport; a trainer or instructor; or, as a verb, 'to educate' or 'to instruct'.

Despite its small size, in the late Middle Ages Kócs became known across Hungary for the quality of its wheelwrights' craftsmanship. In the fifteenth century, local wheel-makers in Kócs began manufacturing expertly made carts and horse-drawn wagons that were sturdily built but still relatively lightweight and utilised an innovative steel-sprung suspension system in their design. This made the *kocsi szeker*, or 'Kócs wagon', a much faster and smoother ride than most comparable vehicles – and, ultimately, the personal cart of choice for Ferdinand I, King of Hungary.

With the royal seal of approval, the Kócs wagon and its innovative sprung suspension soon became popular both within Hungary and far beyond its borders. By the sixteenth century, practically all the major countries and languages of Europe had absorbed the Hungarian *kocsi* into their vocabularies to refer to this new kind of cart. In Polish, it was the *kocz*. In German, it was the *kutsche*. The Italians had the *cocchio*, the Dutch the *koets*. Spain, Portugal and France all had their own local versions of the *coche*. The English finally picked up their word for it from their French neighbours in the mid 1500s, and we've had *coaches* ever since. But this particular story doesn't end there.

Once it had established itself in the language, English speakers began to use the word *coach* as a catch-all term for any similar vehicle or conveyance capable of transporting passengers quickly and in comfort. So, by the early seventeenth century, the captain's apartment on board ship had become known as the *coach*. By the early 1800s, the first railway carriages were known as *coaches*. The first single-decker buses called *coaches* arrived in the 1920s. And the first aircraft added their *coach* class in the late 1940s.

But when a word endures like this in a language, it often doesn't take long for it to begin to be used more figuratively* – and in the case of *coach*, things began to change in the mid nineteenth century.

Originating in the sharp-witted slang of students at Oxford University, in the 1840s *coach* first began to be used as a jocular name for a private tutor or mentor, whose services are taken on in addition to the university's tuition. In that sense, the word

---

* Dickens, for instance, coined the term *slow coach* in *The Pickwick Papers* (1837):

> *And what does this allusion to the slow coach mean? For aught I know, It may be a reference to Pickwick himself, who has most unquestionably been a criminally slow coach during the whole of this transaction.*

referred to someone who will help, like a vehicle, to 'carry' students through their final exams. This meaning quickly caught on: a verb (originally meaning 'to study for examination', then simply 'to tutor') emerged in the mid 1840s, and by the 1880s *coach* had become a widely employed synonym for 'teacher' or 'instructor', used in all manner of fields or pursuits. Every single one of these meanings we owe to a remote village on the Hungarian border.

21

RAKÓW, POLAND

Racovian

The Polish village of Raków, a hundred miles southeast of Łódź, is today home to just over twelve hundred people. Yet at the time this particular etymological story began, way back in the late sixteenth century, Raków was a bustling town with a population of around fifteen thousand. So what happened between then and now? Before we come to how Raków came to earn its place in the dictionary, we need to make a quick thousand-mile detour south, to the Italian city of Siena.

It was there in 1539 that a controversial theologian named Faustus Socinus was born. He was the nephew of an earlier unorthodox theologian named Laelius Socinus, and just like his uncle Faustus was something of a religious firebrand. In his writing and preaching, he rejected many established Catholic beliefs, questioned the legitimacy of the Holy Trinity, shunned the notion of original sin, and held that baptism was necessary only for Christian converts. Denounced as heretic in 1559, he fled to Switzerland and then to Florence, before spending the final decades of his life travelling around Eastern Europe promulgating his own 'Socinian' interpretation of Christian scripture. In the late 1500s, his travels finally brought him to Poland.

Arriving first in Kraków in 1579, Socinus was promptly appointed the leader of a Protestant branch of the Polish church known as the Polish Brethren. The Brethren soon converted to Socinus's new (if somewhat controversial) theology, and under his control this newly defined religious movement spread quickly throughout the country. By the turn of the century, there were several hundred Polish Socinian churches with the movement's intellectual and academic hub focused in the tiny village of Raków.

Raków had been founded only a few decades earlier, but in 1602 the opening of a school in the town for the sole purpose of teaching Socinian theology transformed its prospects. This Racovian Academy, as it was known, was followed soon after by the opening of a local printing press, which soon began churning out countless Socinian books and pamphlets. Within a matter of a few years, Raków grew from a modest village to a bustling university town.

In 1605, the press at Raków published the Racovian Catechism, in which all the tenets of the Socinian movement were formally outlined. With it, word of the town's association with the Socinian movement soon began to spread; the word *Rakovian*, first meaning 'an advocate of Socinian theology', made its debut in English in 1643, albeit in a pamphlet denouncing the *Rise, Growth and Danger of Socinianism*. However, by that time, in its native Poland, the entire movement was beginning to falter.

The Catholic Church's ongoing Counter-Reformation, which sought to redress the Protestant Reformation of the previous century, led to the forced closure of the Racovian Academy and its presses in 1638. Faced with forcibly converting to Catholicism, many of its staff and students instead fled Poland for Socinian enclaves in Romania, Germany, the Netherlands and England. But few of these communities survived more than a few decades, and without its educational and propagandising base in Raków – and with many of its previous advocates now converts or exiles – the Socinian movement collapsed. And with it went the theological term *Racovian*, which by the eighteenth century had largely become consigned to the history books.

But there was one more sting in this etymological tail: the word *Racovian* did not disappear completely. The Socinian movement might have faltered, but so controversial had its tenets been that by the early 1700s the word *Racovian* had established itself as a byword for any follower of an unorthodox or dissenting theology that positioned itself in opposition to established religion or doctrine. Put another way, the word *Racovian* – little known today – had become another word for a heretic.

22

JÁCHYMOV, CZECH REPUBLIC

dollar

F ew of our etymological destinations will have had quite as great an impact on the modern world as the tiny Bohemian spa town of Jáchymov, located high in the Ore mountains that straddle the border between Germany and the Czech Republic. It has given us one of the world's most familiar words. If you've never heard of Jáchymov – or *Joachimsthal*, as it was known until the late 1800s – you won't be alone. Arguably very few people besides its three thousand residents will have done.

Despite being relatively little known, Jáchymov has a number of potential claims to fame, among them the fact that it was in radioactive minerals mined in Jáchymov that the Polish chemist Marie Curie discovered the element radium in 1898. Jáchymov ultimately became the world's foremost producer of radium in the late nineteenth and early twentieth centuries. That distinction came at a price: mining is a dangerous profession at the best of times, but if you're excavating radioactive pitchblende in vast quantities, at a time long before the causes and after-effects of radiation are known, things can turn even nastier. For that reason, even as late as the 1940s the life expectancy in Jáchymov was just forty-two years, but happily there's a lot more in the hills and mountains around Jáchymov than potentially lethal radioactivity.

In the early sixteenth century, silver was discovered in the northwest of what was at the time Bohemia. The town of Joachimsthal was founded in 1516 to support the ever expanding silver mine that sprang up nearby and was to make the local landowners, the Counts von Schlick, one of Bohemia's richest families.

The silver mined in Joachimsthal was of exceptional quality, and in 1525 the Schlicks began to use it to mint their own high-value coins known as *guldengroschens*,* or *guldiners*. The Schlicks' guldiners were embossed on the one side with the traditional heraldic image of a Bohemian lion, and on the other with an image of St Joachim, father of the Virgin Mary and namesake of the valley, or *thal*, in which Joachimsthal stood.

The Schlicks' coins soon caught on, and before long several of the other mining towns in the area had started to mint their own versions and designs. But it was the original that endured: although of varying size and value, all the coins now being made from silver in the area around Joachimsthal came to bear the town's name, and were soon being circulated all across Europe under the name *joachimsthaler*.

The problem with the word *joachimsthaler* is that it's something of a mouthful. And if there's one thing language users don't like, it's words that have arguably just a few too many syllables. While the *joachimsthaler* coins caught on, the word itself did not. Instead it was simplified, so that by the mid sixteenth century these coins had become known merely as *thalers*.

---

* Derived from the German for 'golden groat', the *guldengroschen* was so called because, despite being made of silver, it was intended to have the same value as a *goldgulden*, an earlier denomination of gold coin used in the Holy Roman Empire.

Before long, these thalers were being traded and spent every-where from the Netherlands (where they were known as *daalders*) to Yugoslavia (*tolar*) and Scandinavia (*daler*). In English, the word *thaler* fell into use in the mid 1500s, where it soon adopted the more anglicised spelling by which it would eventually become world-famous. By as early as 1603, the *thaler* had become the *dollar*.

By the turn of the sixteenth century *dollar* had become a byword for any coin of similar value, appearance or size to the original Bohemian *thaler* – chief among which was the Spanish peso (the original 'piece of eight'), which was widely circulated in Britain's burgeoning North American colonies. As these col-onies grew in size and prosperity, these 'Spanish dollars', as they were known, became the go-to currency for trade in North America. Although other currencies with similar names were in use in colonial America (including the Dutch *leeuwendaalder*, or 'lion dollar'), when it came to establishing a new decimal coin-age system for the newly independent United States of America in the early 1780s, it was the Spanish dollar that provided the template:*

> *We cannot use the British pound . . . I therefore propose that the unit of currency of these United States be, across the nation, called the dollar. The unit or [Spanish] dollar is a known coin,*

---

* Ironically neither Thomas Jefferson nor Alexander Hamilton was par-ticularly enamoured of the word *dollar*, and in outlining the laws of the United States used both it and the word *unit* effectively as placeholders, to be replaced with a more permanent term in the future. As professor of anthropology Jack Weatherford wrote in his *History of Money* (1997), the pair 'never suggested an alternative. They wrote the laws to refer to the currency as the *dollar*, or *unit*, apparently with the idea that they would think of a better name later.'

and the most familiar of all to the mind of the people. It is already adopted from south to north.
—Thomas Jefferson, *Notes on the Establishment of a Money Unit, and of a Coinage for the United States* (1784)

It wasn't just the United States, of course: from Canada and Australia to Liberia and the Turks and Caicos Islands, a unit of currency known as the *dollar* is today used in more than fifty countries and territories worldwide. That alone makes its derivation from a tiny Czech mining town all the more extraordinary.

23

KAHLENBERGERDORF, AUSTRIA

calembour

Kahlenbergerdorf, a picturesque district of the Austrian capital Vienna, is believed to be the origin of the little-used word *calembour*, meaning 'pun' or 'play on words', borrowed into English from French in the early nineteenth century. If you think those two words don't look anything alike, you'd be right. They don't. So how did one inspire the other?

One popular explanation is that the missing link here is an otherwise unnamed Count of Kahlenbergerdorf, who, according to a nineteenth-century *Dictionary of Science, Literature and Art*, 'visited Paris in the reign of Louis XV, and was famous for his blunders in the French language'. The French name for Kahlenbergerdorf (or rather, Kalenberg as it was known at the time) was *Calemberg*, and with a little bit of etymological jiggery-pokery, it was this tongue-twisting Count of Calemberg whose name eventually morphed into *calembour*.

It's a neat story, certainly, but alas there's little evidence to back it up. Instead, the more likely explanation here is a much more convoluted tale involving a fourteenth-century Austrian clergyman, a stock character from German theatrical farces, and yet more etymological jiggery-pokery.

The Austrian clergyman in question was one Gundacker von Thernberg, who served as the parish priest of Kahlenbergerdorf from 1339 to 1355. Very little is known about Thernberg's life, but given how he was to become immortalised in the years after his death, we can presume that he was a fairly witty and wily character whose deeds (and maybe misdeeds) earned him quite a reputation. How do we know all that? Well, in the late 1400s, long after Thernberg's death, a Viennese writer named Philipp Frankfurter compiled an anthology of comic tales called *Pfarrer vom Kalenberg* (1473), or the 'Priest of Kahlenberg'. Frankfurter's collection was reportedly based on well-known local anecdotes about a knavish parish priest in Kahlenbergerdorf, who would play practical jokes both on his parishioners and on the members of the nearby Duke of Vienna's court:

> *On one occasion, [the priest] had purchased a quantity of wine, and finding it too bad for his own drinking, he announced that he intended to fly from the steeple of his church across the Danube. A number of peasants collected to witness the miracle. The priest kept them waiting a long while. The day was very hot, the peasants wanted something to drink, and the rector's sour wine went off [i.e. sold] at a famous price. When it was all consumed, the priest appeared, and asked the people whether they had ever seen a man fly? As a universal 'No!' was answered, he continued, 'Well, then, you shall not see me; it is a sinful thing to desire such an extraordinary novelty. Go home – I give you my blessing!' The peasants went away, some laughing, some cursing; but the priest was enabled to buy better wine.*
>
> —'Curiosities of German History', *Ainsworth's Magazine* (1824)

In another story, the priest introduces himself to the local duke, who offers him a gift in return for his loyalty. Oddly, the priest requests a hundred lashes, and gladly accepts fifty of them before pointing out that the duke's gatekeeper had admitted him into the court only if he promised to give him half of whatever gift the duke bestowed on him. To the amusement of the duke – and presumably the priest – the gatekeeper was called for, and promptly awarded his fifty lashes.

Frankfurter's anthology of stories soon proved hugely popular throughout Europe,* and before long the prankster priest of Kahlenberg had become a stock character in German and Austrian literature and comic theatre. A vast catalogue of stories associated with him had soon emerged, and other collections of comic tales demonstrating both the priest's craftiness and his cruel sense of humour began to be published elsewhere.

The name *Kahlenberg* ultimately became a nickname for a wise-cracking anecdotist or practical joker, and it remained in use in this sense long after the tales that had inspired it fell out of fashion.

But with these tales now drifting into obscurity and without their context to support it, the word *Kahlenberg* began to change. In French, it became confused with the word *bourde*, meaning 'blunder' or 'stumble', and in the late eighteenth century a new word entered the language: *calembour*. Combining a word for a wise-cracking comedian with one for someone who literally 'stumbles' or 'blunders' their words together, *calembour* came to be used for a pun or an instance of wordplay, and it was in that sense the word drifted into use in English in the early 1800s. It only remotely caught on and *calembour* has remained something of a linguistic curio ever since.

* Frankfurter did not name the priest who had inspired the stories in his collection, but later writers did. Before long, Gundacker von Thernberg had soon been identified as Kahlenberg's knavish, joke-playing priest.

24

MAGENTA, ITALY

magenta

We now enter Italy, a country in which we're spoilt for etymological choice. Among the countless words and phrases we owe to the Italian map are words as familiar as *jeans*, which take their name from Genoa (where a thick corduroy-like fabric known as *Gene fustian* was once made), and *cantaloupe* melons, which were introduced to Europe from Asia but take their name from *Cantalupo*,* a papal estate outside Rome where they were once grown.

Bergamot takes its name from Bergamo in Lombardy, while *leghorn* chickens namecheck the Tuscan port of Livorno. *Tarantulas* are named after the city of Taranto in southern Italy, where a huge species of wolf spider first became known by that name in the sixteenth century. And the *Rubicon* you proverbially cross when you go too far to turn back is the name of a shallow river that empties into the Adriatic just north of Rimini. Famously, as the river once marked the boundary between Italy proper, Italia, and the Roman province of Cisalpine Gaul, when

---

* *Cantalupo*, incidentally, means 'place of the singing wolf'. No one is entirely sure why, but it's possible the name refers to the fact that the wolves howling in the hills around Rome could be clearly heard there.

Julius Caesar 'crossed the Rubicon' on his way to Rome in 49 BCE, he effectively declared war on the Italian king, Pompey – with no going back.

At the more obscure end of the scale, *sybarites* are lovers of luxury, or hedonistic devotees of pleasure or indulgence, whose name derives from the Ancient Greek colony of Sybaris that once stood on Italy's south coast. *Faience*, a term for glazed earthenware or ceramics, originally referred to a specific type of tin-glazed pottery manufactured in the city of Faenza in Ravenna. And the seldom used but eminently useful adjective *fescennine*, meaning 'obscene' or 'scurrilous', derives from the Ancient Roman city of Fescennia, in modern-day Lazio, whose citizens were apparently known for their bawdy drinking songs and indecent verses.

Italy is also responsible for the names of three colours or pigments: *sienna*, *umber* and *magenta*.

Sienna, or *terra-sienna*, is an earthy reddish-brown colour manufactured originally from the iron-rich clay found around the city of Siena in Tuscany. The name of another earthy orange colour, *umber*, is probably a jumble of the Italian for 'shadow', *ombra*, and the landlocked province of *Umbria* in central Italy. And *magenta* – one of the four basic shades of colour printing, alongside yellow, black and cyan – takes its name from the town of Magenta just outside Milan, in Lombardy, in the far north of Italy.

It was here, on 4 June 1859, that a bloody battle was fought by the allied forces of the French empire and the Sardinian Army against the considerably more sizeable Austrian Army. Under Napoleon III, the French secured a narrow but decisive victory at Magenta. By crossing a nearby river they outflanked the Austrian troops, forcing them to retreat into the surrounding countryside where the French pressed home their advantage. The sweltering hot weather made fighting difficult, while the terrain – a mixture of orchards, streams and irrigation canals – made any of the large-scale military manoeuvres the Austrians excelled at all but impossible. Hand-to-hand fighting with swords and bayonets ultimately dominated the battle, and as the French stormed the nearby town of Magenta, steadily emptying the heavily fortified buildings of their Austrian sharpshooters, they quickly secured their victory.

But what connects this sweltering hand-to-hand battle to the purplish dye we know as *magenta* today? One explanation claims that the colour was a reference to the bloodied uniforms of the French and Austrian troops – but magenta is more of a pinkish-purple shade than it is blood-red, which suggests this might be little more than linguistic folklore. Another theory claims that the French side was vastly fleshed out with hundreds of *zouaves*, light infantrymen of Algerian or North African origin, who were known for wearing a distinctive and often brilliantly coloured uniform of headbands, short open jackets, and bright, crimson-red billowing trousers. But again, crimson isn't magenta and the zouaves were involved in a great many more battles than this one. Instead, as is often the case in etymological conundrums, it seems the most likely theory is also the most straightforward.

The Battle of Magenta came partway through what would eventually become known as the Franco–Austrian War. At the time, much of northern Italy was under Austrian control, but the French victory at Magenta had demonstrated that even this great empire could still be beaten and overthrown. Before long, many towns and cities across the north of Italy had risen up and begun rebelling against Austrian rule; the battle had marked a turning point in the war, and after it the fight to reunify Italy greatly picked up pace.

As it happens, some two hundred and fifty miles west in Lyon, another turning point – a somewhat less momentous one – had been reached. A French chemist named François-Emmanuel Verguin had developed a new bright purple aniline dye, more vivid and potent than any similar dye had been before. Verguin originally named his invention *fuchsine*, after the purplish flowers of the fuchsia shrub that it resembled, but as the dye caught on across France it eventually came to be associated with the name of the staggering French victory that was soon the talk of the country.

Whether Verguin was happy with the name change or not is unknown.* Whether he was or not, the name soon stuck, and *magenta* joined the long list of Italian place names that have since become immortalised in the English dictionary.

---

* Whether the English chemists Chambers Nicolson and George Maule, whom Verguin beat to the discovery of magenta by just a matter of months, were happy with the situation is an easier question to answer.

25

JURA MOUNTAINS, FRANCE/SWITZERLAND

Jurassic

Now for a walk in the mountains – the Jura Mountains to be precise, straddling the border between Switzerland and France. The name *Jura* derives from an ancient Celtic word meaning 'forest', and these tree-covered peaks mark the more verdant western end of the Alps. What brings us here is a term from palaeontology that has been shaped and reshaped over hundreds of millions of years.

There can't be many terms from the geological timeline that have fallen into mainstream use, but *Jurassic* is certainly one – and you can thank the author Michael Crichton and film director Steven Spielberg for that. Crichton's 1990 science fiction novel *Jurassic Park* and its resultant film franchise, in which dinosaurs are reborn using DNA extracted from fossilised mosquitoes, have helped lift a term from fairly obscure geological contexts into practically every English speaker's vocabulary. Certainly, the same can't be said for the word *Jurassic*'s geological contemporaries: *Ordovician Park* doesn't have quite the same ring to it (and, admittedly, a theme park filled with the kinds of primitive molluscs and jawless fish that developed during the Ordovician Period wouldn't be quite as menacing as *Jurassic*

Park's dinosaurs). But if we can thank the success of *Jurassic Park* for the word's familiarity today, who can we thank for the word *Jurassic* itself?

This story begins with the terrifically named Abraham Gottlob Werner, born in Silesia (now in modern-day Poland) in 1749. A mining inspector by trade, in the late 1700s Werner became interested in the differences between the geology of one region and another, and one strata of rocks compared to the others around it.

Quite correctly, he theorised that these different rock formations must correspond to different periods in the history of the Earth. Less accurate was his follow-up theory: that the Earth began life covered in a single vast mineral-rich ocean. This enormous primordial sea, Werner believed, steadily receded over thousands of years while depositing the different rocks that now make up our landscape at different periods in time.

This water-based theory of the Earth's geology fittingly became known as *Neptunism*, after the Roman god of the sea. But eventually it was proved to be misguided, and Neptunism was superseded by better-informed theories in the nineteenth century. Werner's notion that different rock formations corresponded to different geological time periods nevertheless endured – and that brings us to the next character in our story: the Prussian geographer Alexander von Humboldt, born in Berlin in 1769.

Humboldt's contribution to science is so gargantuan that labelling him merely a 'geographer' does not do him justice. Among the countless disciplines his work influenced are geology, botany, zoology, mineralogy, meteorology, geomagnetism, astronomy and navigation, besides which he carved out a career as an explorer, travelling extensively around the Americas on a grand five-year voyage from 1799 to 1804. As a result, everything from a species of South American penguin to a Peruvian sea current have been named in his honour – but it's another contribution to our dictionary that concerns us now.

In 1795, shortly before his American expedition, Humboldt found himself on a tour of the French–Swiss mountains. While out walking one day, he began to contemplate the geology of the region around him and attempted to ally what he saw with Werner's theories. Werner had classified the limestone mountains of Central Europe as *Muschelkalk* – literally 'mussel chalk', a type of seashell-bearing limestone deposited relatively late in Earth's timeline. Humboldt, however, thought otherwise.

'I became convinced,' he later wrote, 'that the Jura limestone . . . was a distinct formation', isolated between a distinct layer of older gypsum above it, and newer sandstone below. This 'Jurassic' limestone did not fit with Werner's theory and so, Humboldt believed, must have been formed at a different period of time.

Later geologists picked up on Humboldt's ideas, and began to identify ever more subtle differences between Werner's original classifications. Eventually, an entirely new classification of rock was established – along with an entirely new stage of geological time, with its own fossil record and unique flora and fauna. Thanks to Humboldt's Alpine holiday, it took a name honouring the Jura mountains: the *Jurassic* period, as we now know it, had finally arrived.

26

MONTE CARLO, MONACO

Monte Carlo fallacy

I n the mid 1850s, with his principality almost bankrupt, the then prince of Monaco, Charles III, was compelled to grant a licence permitting a pair of local businessmen, Albert Aubert and Napoleon Langlois, to open and begin operating two new commercial enterprises on the Monaco seafront.* One was a health resort specialising in thalassotherapy, the use of seawater in the healing and treatment of various diseases. The other was a casino complex. One of these businesses proved considerably more successful than the other. And no, this isn't an entry dedicated to the origin of the word *thalassotherapy*.†

The casino opened in 1863, and after a troublesome few years quickly helped the tiny principality to turn its fortunes around.

---

* While we're here, the etymology of the name *Monaco* is worth noting: it derives from the Greek words for 'one' or 'single', *monos*, and 'house', *oikos*. *Monoikos*, or 'single-house', was an epithet of the great hero Heracles, who is supposed by legend to have passed through Monaco on his travels. The temple of *Heracles Monoikos* was built there in his name, and we've known this tiny enclave of France as Monaco ever since.

† Spoiler alert: it's from *thalassa*, a Greek word for 'sea'.

The cash-rich district that developed around the complex became known as Monte Carlo – Italian for 'Charles' mountain' – in honour of the prince who had kickstarted the entire enterprise.

So successful was the Monte Carlo development that its name, and indeed that of Monaco as a whole, soon fell into use in various money-related contexts in nineteenth-century slang. By the late 1800s, a *monte** or *monty* was a sure thing – a bet destined to pay off. In French slang, *monaco* became a slang name for cash or loose change, or else a low-denomination coin that could be spent or gambled without being missed. But the term that brings us here now is the name of a theory outlined in the 1950s to account for a notoriously misjudged example of gam-blers' reasoning: the *Monte Carlo fallacy*.

Also known simply as the 'gambler's fallacy' (or, if you want to be technical, the 'fallacy of maturing chances'), the *Monte Carlo fallacy* explains the misguided belief some people develop that, just because something has happened *less* frequently than might be expected, it is now *more* likely to occur.

Imagine that a coin is tossed ten times in a row, and every single time, bar none, it lands on heads. To some observers, that peculiar run of heads might seem too unusual to ignore – and make it seem that the coin landing on tails is now somehow 'over-due', and more likely on the next flip or, at least, sooner rather than later. But as everyone knows, every coin toss carries a 50/50 chance of *either* heads *or* tails. With that in mind, and with each flip taken in isolation, a run of ten heads in a row doesn't seem all that unusual, and certainly wouldn't do anything to alter the odds of tails coming up next.

---

* In his *Dictionary of Slang and Unconventional English* (1937) the lexicog-rapher Eric Partridge pointed out that the name *Monte* was also used as a slang nickname for Monte Carlo as a whole, but 'mostly by those who have never been there'.

However misguided, this presumption is nevertheless a common trait: us humans are hard-wired to look for and appreciate patterns, and in doing so find any perceived imbalances (like ten heads in a row) worthy of note. And it is this pattern-seeking behaviour that led to this entire phenomenon earning itself a nickname namechecking Monte Carlo, the gambling capital of Europe.

On 18 August 1913, a game of roulette at the Monte Carlo casino attracted more than its usual share of the local gamblers' attention. In fact, the entire building was abuzz with the fact that on one of the roulette tables, black numbers had come up fifteen – then sixteen, seventeen and eighteen – times in a row. In all, the ball went on to land on a black number some twenty-six consecutive times – and the longer this streak of black numbers continued, the more the gamblers around the table began to be suckered in to the fallacy. Surely, they began to wager, a red number was now due?

The fact that each spin of the roulette wheel, just like the flip of a coin, has a roughly equal chance of landing on red or black did not matter. Bet after bet was placed, and as the run of black numbers continued, the wagers on red grew ever larger. Millions of francs were placed and lost as more and more players bought into the misguided assumption that this uncommon – but not impossible – run of black numbers had at some point to be balanced out by a red number.

Eventually, of course, a red number did appear. And by then, presumably, the players had learned a very valuable and very expensive lesson.

27

PORTO,
PORTUGAL

port

From Monte Carlo, we're heading as far west as it's possible to go in mainland Europe: Portugal.

England and Portugal are two of the world's oldest allies – if not indeed the oldest of all. On 16 June 1373, the two nations, represented by Edward III of England and King Ferdinand and Queen Eleanor of Portugal, signed an Anglo-Portuguese Treaty that united the two countries in 'faithfully obeying, true, faithful, constant, mutual, and perpetual friendships, unions, alliances, and leagues of sincere affection'. The treaty is considered the oldest active treaty of its kind in the world.*

---

* The alliance endured long enough for Portugal to agree to Britain establishing a major Allied naval base on the Portuguese-controlled islands of the Azores, in the north Atlantic Ocean, in 1943. The agreement was ratified by Prime Minister Winston Churchill, who recalled his announcement of the arrangement in his multi-volume history of the Second World War:

> 'I have an announcement,' I said, 'to make to the House, arising out of the treaty signed between this country and Portugal in the year 1373, between

As long-standing friends and allies, surely Portugal will fare well in the English language, and won't fall victim to the same snide sideswipes and stereotypes that coloured, say, the Dutch entry in this book? Well . . .

In his 1929 collection of *Sea Slang*, the lexicographer Frank C. Bowen explained that sailors in the nineteenth century used the designation *Portuguese* as 'the old Navy name for all foreigners except Frenchmen'. Insulting, yes, but perhaps more revealingly uncomplimentary to the British than to anyone else. Another maritime expression, *Portugee devil* [*sic*], was defined somewhat openly in an 1840 edition of the *London Saturday Journal* as something that 'when good [is] too good'. Wilfred Granville's *Dictionary of Sailors' Slang* (1962) explained that to Victorian seafarers a *Portuguese parliament* was 'a rowdy discussion in which everybody talks and nobody listens' – perhaps a reference either to the noisy outspokenness of Portuguese recruits, or to the relative indecipherability of the Portuguese language to English ears.

And then there's James Redding Ware's dictionary of *Passing English of the Victorian Era*, in which he recorded an entry for a *Portuguese pumping*. Ominously flagging it as an expression 'not to be learnt', Ware explains:

> *Ask sailors the meaning of this phrase, and they may laugh a good deal, but they give no etymology. It is probably nasty.*
> —J. R. Ware, *Passing English of the Victorian Era* (1909)

> *His Majesty King Edward III and King Ferdinand and Queen Eleanor of Portugal.' I spoke in a level voice, and made a pause to allow the House to take in the date, 1373. As this soaked in there was something like a gasp. I do not suppose any such continuity of relations between two Powers has ever been, or will ever be, set forth in the ordinary day-to-day work of British diplomacy.*
> —Winston Churchill, *The Second World War* (1948–53)

'Nasty' was the word, all right: in his later *Dictionary of Unconventional English*, Eric Partridge wrote that the phrase 'refers almost certainly to either defecation . . . or to masturbation'.* As the American lexicographer (and Harvard professor of psychology) A. A. Roback put it in his *Dictionary of the International Slurs* (1944), perhaps this is best defined as 'a phrase of uncertain but unquestionably questionable meaning'.

Happily, however, there's more to the Portuguese–English story than thinly veiled xenophobia and questionable pumping. Among the words English speakers owe to their oldest allies is also one of the most obvious: the Portuguese gave us *port*.

Not *port* in the sense of a safe harbour, of course; it dates back to the Old English period, and has its roots in a Latin word meaning 'entrance' or 'refuge'. Nor *port* in the naval context, meaning 'opposite of starboard,† as it merely helped to identify the side of a vessel more often than not facing the harbour when it is docked. The *port* we owe to Portugal is the sweet, dark-red wine, which was first described in the English language in the early seventeenth century.

In this context, it's thought the name *port* probably first referred simply to any red wine brought into England via Porto, the major port city on Portugal's north coast. When trade with the likes of France, the Netherlands and Germany became

---

* Later dictionaries of slang have tended to side with the latter of these two possibilities, although Partridge, adding that 'pumping ship' was once a nautical euphemism for urination, seemed to suggest the former was more likely.

† Oddly, this *port* was originally known as *larboard*, until an official Order of the Admiralty in 1844 replaced one name with the other to avoid the (presumably quite considerable) confusion between the two. Etymologically, the *starboard* side is literally the side on which a vessel is steered (from Old English *steor*, 'rudder'); the *larboard* side was the usual loading side (from Old English *hladan*, 'to load, to burden').

disrupted by conflict during the eighteenth and nineteenth centuries, trade from England's allies in Portugal picked up apace to cover the shortfall, and *port* wines became more popular. Brandy was often mixed with the wine to help preserve it during the lengthy shipping time, but when this enriched taste proved even more popular than the red wine itself, the port began to be deliberately fortified with the spirit during the fermentation process. Port as we know it – and drink it – today was born.

28

JEREZ DE LA FRONTERA, SPAIN

sherry

The southern Spanish city of Jerez de la Frontera is the namesake of *sherry*, another fortified wine made from grapes grown in and around the city, in southwest Andalusia. Viticulture there dates back into antiquity, but the large-scale production and export of sherry and other similar wines from the south of Spain did not develop until considerably later. By the fifteenth century, however, sherry was being enjoyed all across Europe, and far, far beyond: Columbus famously took a cargo of sherry with him on his voyage to the New World in 1492, and when Ferdinand Magellan began his circumnavigation of the world in 1519, he had more than two hundred and fifty kegs of sherry in the hold to sustain him and his crew.*

---

* Magellan had the right idea: in preparing for his trip, he spent more money on wine than on weaponry.

In England, sherry grew in popularity after the Andalusian port of Cadiz was sacked by Francis Drake in 1587; among the spoils, Drake brought almost three thousand barrels of sherry back with him to Britain. It was around this time that the word first appeared in English, although not in the form we know it today. Initially, sherry was known as *sherris* – the name by which it appeared in Shakespeare's *Henry IV Part 2*:

> *A good sherris-sack hath a twofold operation in it. It ascends me into the brain, dries me there all the foolish and dull and crudy vapours which environ it, makes it apprehensive, quick, forgetive, full of nimble, fiery, and delectable shapes, which, delivered o'er to the voice, the tongue, which is the birth, becomes excellent wit. The second property of your excellent sherris is the warming of the blood, which before, cold and settled, left the liver white and pale, which is the badge of pusillanimity and cowardice. But the sherry warms it, and makes it course from the inwards to the parts' extremes.*
> —*Henry IV Part 2* (IV.iii)

The spelling *sherris* represents an anglicised version of *Jerez* (which at the time was known by the Spanish name of *Xeres*), and was pronounced precisely as it's written: '*sheh*-riss', rhyming with *Ferris*. So how did we get from *sherris* to *sherry*?

If you put an S at the end of a word in English, people are going to think that it's plural. That's how we ended up with the word *pea* from the original singular form *pease*, and misconstrued the singular word *statistic* from the plural field of *statistics*. Likewise, *sherris*, with its final S, was misinterpreted as a plural repeatedly enough for an erroneous singular form, *sherry*, to surface around the turn of the sixteenth–seventeenth century. *Sherris*, meanwhile, remained in occasional use right through to the 1800s, but eventually *sherry* established itself as the dominant form and we've been drinking it ever since.

29

GIBRALTAR

Siege of Gibraltar

From Jerez, we head southeast, across Andalusia, and on to Gibraltar, the tiny 2.6-square-mile British-owned territory on the very southernmost tip of Europe's Iberian peninsula. From here, you can see across the Straits of Gibraltar to Africa, which lies barely eight nautical miles away across the Mediterranean Sea. With all this talk of *port* and *sherry*, perhaps it's time for a quick toast?

If someone were to ask you what year the Siege of Gibraltar took place, what would you say? If you answered 1779, then kudos to you. If you answered, 'which one?', then even better; you're obviously a genius. Or a naval historian.

The fact is that Gibraltar occupies such a strategically formidable position on the European mainland that it has been invaded, bombarded and besieged on no fewer than fourteen separate occasions throughout history – from the First Siege of Gibraltar in 1309, which saw the Moors hand control of the area to the Kingdom of Castile, to the last and so-called Great Siege, which lasted for four years, 1779–83. That violent history can't have been much fun for the locals, it has to be said, but it does at least have a silver lining: the sailors of the British Navy managed to get a joke out of it.

In eighteenth-century naval slang, anyone who fancied a drink but could not think of a good enough excuse to have one – or, alternatively, anyone caught having a drink and questioned why they were on the booze at whatever time they were discovered – would reply that they were commemorating 'the anniversary of the Siege of Gibraltar'. The joke was that given the sheer number of them in the military history books, it was fairly likely that regardless of the date, there was an anniversary of at least *one* siege of Gibraltar coming up sometime soon. Before long, the expression *the Siege of Gibraltar* had slipped into English slang as an excuse for a drink, whether warranted or not. It's five o'clock somewhere, after all.

30

TANGIER, MOROCCO

tangerine

We might be on a different continent now, but as the crow flies we've travelled only thirty-six miles. We've arrived in Tangier – the third-largest and northernmost city in Morocco, on Africa's far northwest coast.

As we'll soon discover, African place names in our language are fairly thin on the ground (especially compared with the etymological gold we were able to mine back in Europe). But of all the African nations, Morocco has more to offer us than most.

The instantly recognisable *fez* hat, for instance, apparently owes its existence to the Moroccan city of the same name. At least one theory about the origin of the *ouija* board is that it takes its name (via some suitably mysterious connection) from the city of Oujda, close to the Morocco–Algeria border.* And

* A more commonly held explanation of the word *ouija* is that it's a seemingly random amalgamation of the French and German words for 'yes', *oui* and *ja*. This is by no means a watertight theory, however, and the similarity between *ouija* and the city of Oujda certainly can't be

even Morocco itself has given its name to a type of light, flexible leather; through punning confusion between this *morocco* leather, *buff* leather, and *buff* as a colloquialism for 'nakedness', *to be in your morocco* meant 'to be unclothed' in nineteenth-century slang.

None of these words and phrases are what has brought us to Tangier, however. Instead, we're here for the humble *tangerine*. When it first appeared in the English language in the early eighteenth century, *tangerine* was an adjective merely describing anything deriving from or akin to the city of Tangier. By the 1800s, however, a smaller, sweeter-tasting variety of orange was beginning to appear in English fruit bowls originating in the orange groves of northern Africa. Squatter and less round in shape than an ordinary orange, the fruit became known as the *tangerine* in honour of the Atlantic port from which they were imported into Britain; the earliest known reference to a *tangerine* orange dates from 1842.

But just as there was no word in English for the colour orange until oranges began to be imported into England in the Middle Ages, not long after tangerines began to appear

discounted. According to a popular tale from occult folklore, however, the ouija board actually named itself.

At a seance in Baltimore held by one of the ouija board's inventors, Charles Kennard, in 1890, the then unnamed board was reportedly asked what it would like to call itself; in response, it spelled out the letters O–U–I–J–A. When the group then asked what that word meant, the board supposedly replied, 'GOOD LUCK'. It was only after the seance was over that one of the attendees, Baltimore socialite Helen Peters Nosworthy, opened a locket that she was wearing around her neck to reveal a picture of a young woman with the name OUIDA written beneath it. Peters, it transpired, was a fan of the British novelist Maria Louise de la Ramée, who published a number of best-selling romance and adventure books in the late nineteenth century under the pen name 'Ouida'; the coincidence, regardless of the curious misspelling, was too strange to ignore.

in England the word *tangerine* itself became the name of a deep shade of orange, darker and richer in tone than other similar colours. In this context, the word was first used in 1899, and both it and the fruit from which it derives have remained in common use ever since.

31

ALGIERS, ALGERIA

Algerine

From *tangerines*, to *Algerines*. With a capital A, the word *Algerine* is a fairly old-fashioned word for an inhabitant of Algeria. Dating from the mid seventeenth century in English, *Algerine* has now been all but entirely replaced by the more familiar *Algerian* – which is perhaps for the best, as in the nineteenth century the word picked up an unusual and oddly negative connotation:

> *Algerines (theatrical), performers who bully the manager of a theatre when the salaries are not paid. Also petty money-borrowers.*
> —Albert Barrère and Charles Godfrey Leland,
> *A Dictionary of Slang, Jargon and Cant* (vol. 1, 1889)

So how, or why, did *Algerine* come to be another word for a harrying money-chaser – or, as another dictionary of nineteenth-century slang put it, a 'hard-up borrower of petty sums'? Well, perhaps the answer lies in an even earlier definition from English slang:

*Rum gaggers. Cheats who tell wonderful stories of their sufferings
at sea, or when taken by the Algerines.*
—Francis Grose, *A Classical Dictionary of the Vulgar
Tongue* (1785)

Thanks to its location on Africa's Mediterranean coast, Algeria
gained a reputation for piracy in the seventeenth and eighteenth
centuries. As a result, the 'Algerines' that harry the dishonest
'rum gaggers' described here by Francis Grose are not merely
Algerian nationals, but bloodthirsty pirates and seafaring ban-
dits.* From there, the term fell into theatrical slang, and so it's
likely that the *Algerines* braying at the stage manager's door were
merely being likened to the money-hunting pirates who would
once have chased down merchant ships in the Mediterranean.
(Although it's tempting to think that perhaps an actor who played
a piratical *Algerine* in some nineteenth-century stage play might
have been especially good at extracting the cast's dues.)

As with its western neighbour Morocco, we don't owe an
awful lot of our language to Algeria but compared to some of the
other countries on the African continent, it has given us more
than we might expect.

Bougie, for instance, is an eighteenth-century word for a wax
candle, whose name is an anglicised corruption of the name of the
wax-producing city of Béjaïa on Algeria's Mediterranean coast. A
jazerant or *jesserant* was a light suit of armour from the medieval
period; probably of Moorish or Saracen origin, its name derives
from the Arabic name for Algiers, *al-Jazair*.† And *mazagran* is

---

* Likewise, a *dommerer*, according to Grose, was 'a beggar pretending
that his tongue has been cut out by the Algerines'.
† *Al-Jazair* literally means 'the islands' in Arabic – a reference to a small
chain of four islets lying off (and now partly connected to) the coast of
Algiers. Curiously, Algeria takes its name from its capital city, Algiers, not
the other way around. When the region fell under French rule in 1830,

a traditional Algerian iced coffee, or else the thick earthenware vessel in which it's served, its name commemorating the Battle of Mazagran in 1840, around the same time that the drink became popular among French troops in North Africa.

Algiers was chosen as its capital and the surrounding area was named *Algeria* after it.

32

CANARY ISLANDS

canary

A dozen or so destinations ago we found out all about turkeys, and how they took their name (mistakenly) from Turkey. And before we head south across the Sahara Desert, we have just enough time for one more of these chicken-and-egg – or, rather, turkey-and-egg – etymological tales. From Algeria we head southwest, back across Morocco, to an archipelago of seven islands and countless smaller islets roughly sixty miles off Africa's north Atlantic coast. So which came first, the *canary* bird, or the *Canary* Islands?

The islands were named first: references to what were once known as the *Canariae insulae* have been unearthed in Roman Latin documents dating as far back as the early fourth century. The *canary* birds that inhabited them understandably came to be known only much later. After the islands were settled by European colonists in the fourteenth century, these birds began to be brought back to the mainland to be kept as pets and in menageries, and with them came the name of the islands they inhabited. The earliest reference to one of these *canary birds*, ultimately in English, dates from 1562.

With their bright song, equally bright character, and even brighter yellow plumage, these Canary Island *canaries* quickly proved popular. And as they became ever more familiar to English speakers, their name came to be used in ever broader and more figurative senses.

In late-sixteenth-century slang, for instance, a *canary* was a convict – a punning reference to a 'jailbird' held in a cage. Shakespeare used the word *canary* as a verb in *Love's Labour's Lost*, meaning 'to dance in a lively manner'.* By the eighteenth century, a *canary* was a bright golden coin, such as a sovereign or golden guinea, and by the nineteenth century, a *canary* was a jocular nickname for a soprano singer, on account of her high-pitched song, as well as a nickname for a yellow-uniformed criminal facing transportation to Australia.

The first criminals to *sing like a canary* meanwhile – and thereby confess to their crimes, or rat on their accomplices – did so in the early 1900s, around the same time that earliest figurative reference to a *canary in a coalmine* also appeared in the language.†

---

* It's likely that Shakespeare intended his use of the verb canary to refer both to a dance called the canary that was popular at the time and to the canary bird's sprightliness.

† The practice of coal miners taking a canary with them below ground as a means of detecting poisonous gases was the brainchild of the Scottish chemist John Scott Haldane, who first proposed the idea in the late 1800s. A canary (or a white mouse, as Haldane also suggested) would succumb to any poisonous emanations long before they could cause any serious harm to the mineworkers, and as such essentially operated as an early warning system; the idea was so ingeniously effective that it was not entirely phased out in British coalmines until 1986. By the turn of the nineteenth century, however, the practice had inspired the expression 'a canary in a coalmine', meaning 'an early warning or indicator', or 'something that can be sacrificed early for the sake of the greater good'.

So the birds, it seems, take their name from the islands – but this story isn't quite complete just yet. If the birds are named after the islands, where on earth did the islands take their name from?

Well, that Latin name, *Canariae insulae*, has long puzzled etymologists. One explanation is that the islands were first inhabited and ultimately named after an ancient Berber tribe called the *Canarii*, who are believed to have lived along the West African coast. That's certainly a plausible theory, but according to Pliny the Elder, the islands' true name lies elsewhere.

According to Pliny, there existed an Atlantic island called *Canaria insula* that was apparently so called because of the 'multitude of dogs of a huge size' that inhabited it. Pliny's *Canaria* is now believed to have been Gran Canaria (which, despite its name, is actually the third-largest island in the Canary Islands group). If his account is true, then the Canary Islands presumably take their name from the Latin word *canarius*, the adjectival form of the noun *canis*, meaning 'dog'. And that, despite its name, would essentially make Gran Canaria the original Isle of Dogs.

33

TIMBUKTU, MALI

Timbuktu

There are a number of fairly remote locations on our round-the-world itinerary, but few are quite so out of the way as our next stop. In fact, the town of Timbuktu in Mali has become so well known for its remoteness that its name has drifted into fairly regular use in English as a byword for any impossibly or inconveniently distant location – or, according to the *Oxford English Dictionary*, 'the most distant place imaginable'.

To be fair, it has a point. The town of Timbuktu or *Tombouctou** stands almost at the exact centre of the Republic of Mali in northern Africa. Almost 60 per cent of Mali is covered by the southern Sahara Desert, and the town, and indeed the entire Timbuktu region of which it is the capital, lies deep in the heart of sub-Saharan Africa.† The River Niger drifts by only

---

* The town apparently has a great many English spellings: besides *Timbuktu*, it can be called *Tinbuktu*, *Tumbutu*, Timbuktoo, and Timbuctoo – the latter of which inspired D. H. Lawrence to coin the adjective *Timbuctoot* in 1930, to mean 'originating or only occurring in some out-landish, imagined location'.

† The Timbuktu district in which the town of Timbuktu is located is the largest and northernmost of Mali's ten administrative regions. But it is

a few miles south of the town, but due north there is little else but empty desert for the next thousand miles, with few settlements of any size lying between it and the Mediterranean coastline at Morocco.

Given that kind of isolation, how did Timbuktu come to be known so far outside Mali – let alone find itself a place in our dictionary?

There has been some kind of permanent settlement at Timbuktu* since the twelfth century at least. Originally a native Tuareg encampment, it soon established itself as an important rest stop on the Saharan trade routes of the early Middle Ages, and developed quickly from a small village to a bustling trade town first recorded on European maps in the late 1300s. It reached its peak as part of the Songhai empire, one of ancient Africa's grandest ruling states, in the mid fifteenth century: already wealthy and prosperous, the opening of one of the Islamic world's most important universities in Timbuktu further established it as a major seat of medieval learning, bringing more people, wealth and prosperity to the region. But by the early 1600s, Timbuktu's fortunes were starting to change.

also its hottest, its most desert-covered, and – despite being a little under 200,000 square miles in size – one of its least populated, with a population of roughly 700,000 people. By comparison, imagine the entire population of Leeds living in an area the size of Spain.

* No one is entirely sure why Timbuktu is called *Timbuktu*. One theory claims the name might mean 'wall' or 'hollow' in the local Songhai language, while another suggests it derives from a Berber word meaning 'sand dune', or 'hidden place'. But perhaps most likely of all is the theory that it derives from the name of an aged Tuareg slave woman, who was routinely tasked with guarding the Tuaregs' camp while they roamed the surrounding desert. The woman's name, *Tomboutou*, is said to have meant 'mother with a large navel'.

Competition with other towns and cities in North Africa began to affect Timbuktu's prospects, while trade with Europe faltered as the continent became increasingly reliant on faster and more reliable trade routes with its colonies in the New World rather than Africa. As a result, the town began to dwindle. Its wealth vanished, its people moved elsewhere, and by the time the first European explorers arrived in the town in the nineteenth century, Timbuktu was a shadow of its former self.

Nevertheless, that lengthy period of prosperity had established the town's standing on an international stage for good. Tales of an El Dorado in the desert – an almost mythically prosperous town born out of the sands of the Sahara – had become well known across Europe, lending an air of mystique to the town, while its quirky and oddly rhythmical and idiosyncratic name (to European ears, at least) doubtless helped reinforce its place in European consciousness. All these factors together helped earn the name *Timbuktu* its place in the language, and it first began to be used for any remotely far-flung, edge-of-the-world location in the late nineteenth century.

Being synonymous with isolation and an almost legendary level of inaccessibility has its drawbacks, however. When an appeal to raise the town's profile was launched in 2006, and bids were welcomed to assign the town a British twin, a survey of 150 British people found that two-thirds of them believed Timbuktu was a mythical place, while the remainder thought it didn't exist at all. Well, at least we've got the postcard to prove them wrong.

34

CONAKRY, GUINEA

guinea

From sand-baked Timbuktu, we head almost nine hundred miles southwest to Conakry, the capital of Guinea, on Africa's more temperate western coast.

We're stopping here in the Guinean capital, but we could just have easily have told this next etymological tale two hundred miles up the coast, in Guinea-Bissau. Or more than fifteen hundred miles east, in Equatorial Guinea. Or, in fact, in a boat anywhere off the west coast of central Africa, in the Gulf of Guinea, or the Guinea Bight. That's because it's not Conakry that concerns us here, but rather the somewhat convoluted story of the word *guinea* itself.

To British English speakers, the word *guinea* is probably most familiar as the name of a gold coin, first minted in 1663, that was originally equal in value to one pound sterling, or 20 shillings. As the price of gold fluctuated, so too did the coin's value, rising to 25 shillings by 1668, and peaking at 30 shillings in the late seventeenth century.

Eventually fixed at a value of 21 shillings, the guinea remained in production right through to 1813, but even after it was taken out of circulation its name long remained in colloquial use in British English for the sum of 21 shillings, or £1.05. As a case in point, here is an anecdote from 1980 from comedy actor Kenneth Williams about his habitually acid-tongued friend, Dame Maggie Smith:

> *Kenneth Williams was Maggie's closest friend in her early days. He recounted how, when they were going round Fortnum's together, Maggie was aghast at the prices in the lingerie department. 'Seven guineas for a bra?' she exploded. 'Cheaper to have your tits off!'*
> —Michael Coveney, *Maggie Smith: A Biography* (2015)

But why name it a *guinea* at all?

Although the coin eventually fell into domestic use, when the guinea was first introduced in the 1660s, the Royal Mint intended it to be merely 'for the use of the Company of Royal Adventurers of England trading with Africa'. Embossed with an image of an elephant, these coins – 44½ of which contained one troy pound gold – were to be employed exclusively in Britain's trade with West Africa. It was to facilitate trade along this Guinean coastline that the original *guinea* coins were minted, and eventually earned their name.

Guinea might appear in the names of only a handful of African nations' names today, but geographically it once referred to the entire region that lies along the Gulf of Guinea, the broad arm of the Atlantic Ocean that follows Africa's western coast. How the region earned this name is debatable; perhaps a corruption of some native name (a Tuareg word, *aginaw*, meaning 'dark-skinned people' is one suggestion), the true origins of *guinea* remain a mystery.

One last question remains, then: what on earth is a *guinea pig*?

Unlike turkeys and canaries, guinea pigs don't come from Guinea, but rather from South America (and nor, for that matter, are they pigs). The origin of their name is as mysterious as that of

Guinea itself, with various suggestions claiming it alludes either to the fact they were introduced to Europe aboard *Guinea-men*, a seventeenth-century name for the ships that sailed the Europe–West Africa trade route, or else that they were thought to resemble (more in colour than shape) the Guinean red river hog, a pig native to tropical West Africa.

35

BRAZZAVILLE, CONGO

conga

J ust as the name *Guinea* crops up in the names of several countries but also once referred to a great swathe of the African
continent, the name *Congo* appears in the name of both
the Republic of the Congo (in whose capital, Brazzaville,
we find ourselves briefly now) and the considerably larger
Democratic Republic of the Congo (known as Zaïre until 1997).
Geographically, it also refers to the lush rainforest at the great
green heart of Africa, which fills and surrounds the enormous
Congo River basin.

And just as *Guinea*, in the form of a *guinea pig*, eventually
came to be erroneously attached to something that actually originated on the other side of the Atlantic, in the early 1900s Africa's
Congo basin gave its name to a dance that found its way onto
Western dance floors not from Africa, but from six thousand
miles away in northern Latin America.

The drunken staple of countless office parties, the *conga* is
defined by the *Oxford English Dictionary* as a dance 'usually performed by several people in single file, and consisting of three
steps forward followed by a kick'. It was first described in
English back in the 1930s (when a 1935 edition of a magazine

called *Dancing Times* helpfully explained that 'the conga is not a ball-room dance'), but it is likely that the dance itself developed slightly earlier than that date would suggest.

The name *conga* is thought to come from American Spanish (either via Spanish speakers in the United States, or via Latin America) and began life as the *danza conga*, or literally 'the dance of the Congo'. It's possible that this rowdy, beat-driven dance genuinely has its origins in African tribal rituals; tellingly, a *Congo dance*, performed by African slaves in the southern states of North America, was recorded in American English in the early nineteenth century. But it's just as likely that the name was concocted only to give the impression that the dance had some kind of ancient or ritualistic origin in the tropical heart of Africa. Whatever its true origins, however, either erroneously or genuinely, it was the Congo that gave us the *conga*.

36

STELLENBOSCH, SOUTH AFRICA

Stellenbosch

From Brazzaville, we travel almost two thousand miles south, crossing Angola and Namibia, and on to a small town not far inland from South Africa's Atlantic coast.

After Cape Town, which lies roughly thirty miles to the west, Stellenbosch is the second-oldest European settlement in South Africa's Western Cape province. Established in 1679, it was named after its founder, Simon van der Stel, the first governor of Dutch Cape Colony (which had itself been established only in the early 1650s).

Stellenbosch remained a Dutch colony until the late 1700s, when a turbulent few decades saw both it and the Cape Colony as a whole change hands several times between the Dutch and the British. The British finally established complete control in 1814, and Stellenbosch remained under British rule until South Africa's independence in 1961.

Towards the end of the nineteenth century, however, British rule in South Africa was challenged: the Anglo-Boer War of 1899–1902 saw two Boer-controlled states, the Transvaal and the Orange Free State, rise up against the British colonists in the

Cape. And it was during this time that the town of Stellenbosch earned itself a permanent place in our language.

A British remount camp – a military encampment set aside for the purchase, training, medical care and upkeep of war horses – was established in Stellenbosch at the outbreak of the war. This was long before the days of tanks, jeeps and other motorised military transport, and looking after the army's horses was an important task in turn-of-the-century warfare. The camp was overseen by a revolving staff of British officers. Despite the horse's welfare being of utmost importance to the future conduct of the war, the officers' appointment to the Stellenbosch camp was less an indication of respect, and more evidence of their misconduct.

During the course of the war, officers whose strategies or conduct had not proved successful on the battlefield would find themselves relieved of front-line duty, sent to Stellenbosch, and there tasked with the considerably more behind-the-scenes responsibility of managing the camp. As the horses were imperative to the future of the war, the officers could not be said to have been demoted, but rather moved aside: the work was important, but by no means front-line duty, and those who worked at the Stellenbosch camp knew it. Before long, to be *Stellenbosched* had entered British Army slang:

> *Stellenboshed [sic] . . . to be relegated, as the result of incompetence, to a position in which little harm can be done.*
> —Charles Pettman, *Africanderisms* (1913)

In the sense explained above, *Stellenbosch* is first recorded as early as 1900 (in a *Daily Express* article written by Rudyard Kipling), implying that this meaning established itself in the jargon of the British troops in South Africa almost immediately after the outbreak of the war. Over time it came to be used ever more loosely to mean 'to remove from office', but the stricter sense – of a subtle sidelining of someone, to an important but considerably less impactful position – remained the word's truer meaning.

In that sense, the word remains criminally underused in English today.

37

MOCHA, YEMEN

mocha

From Stellenbosch we head northeast, up Africa's Indian Ocean coast and on to the Red Sea, sandwiched between the African mainland and the Arabian Peninsula.

The far southwest corner of the Arabian Peninsula is occupied by the Arab Republic of Yemen. And the far southwest corner of Yemen in turn sits on a narrow thirty-mile sea strait, linking the Red Sea to the Gulf of Aden, called *Bab-el-Mandeb*, or the 'Gate of Tears' – an ominous reference to the number of ships that have been lost there. Here, on the Yemeni side of the Gate of Tears, is the port city of Mocha.

No prizes for guessing that it's from Mocha that *mocha* coffee takes its name: *Coffea arabica*, the plant from which the arabica coffee bean is obtained, is native to this corner of Arabia, and has been cultivated in Yemen since medieval times. These coffee beans were then dried and transported to the coast for trade. Thanks to Mocha's ideal location on the far southwestern tip of the Arabian Peninsula, during the seventeenth and eighteenth centuries it established itself as arguably the most important coffee-trading port in the world.

Before then, the coffee trade into and out of Mocha had been tightly controlled by the occupying Ottoman Empire. But when the Ottomans withdrew from the far south of Arabia in the early 1600s, trade with the rest of the world flourished – and with it, coffee suddenly became a desirable commodity worldwide.

It wasn't until the eighteenth century that Mocha coffee first began to be described in English texts, but it nevertheless quickly gained a reputation for being among the finest coffee produced anywhere in the world.* As the English philosopher Jeremy Bentham wrote as early as 1793: 'Coffee, to be drinkable, must be made from mocha.'

* Nowadays, the name *mocha* is less associated with the Yemeni strain of coffee beans, and more with a drink made by mixing freshly ground mocha coffee with steamed milk and powdered chocolate. This *mocha* made its debut on coffee-shop menus in 1977.

38

CAIRO, EGYPT

fustian

Egypt, in Africa's far northeast corner, has given our language more than a dozen words, ranging from the familiar to the extraordinary.

The 'gyp–' in *gypsy*, for instance, derives from *Egypt*, as it was from North Africa that these nomadic Romany* peoples were once believed to have originated. *Memphian stone*, or *memphite*, is a legendary gemstone supposed to have magical healing or anaesthetic powers, and is said to originate near to the ancient Egyptian capital of Memphis. The mixture of Greek and Egyptian inscriptions that cover the *Rosetta stone*, discovered by French soldiers in the port city of Rosetta in 1799, famously provided the key to deciphering Egyptian hieroglyphics. Its name ultimately came to be used allusively, to describe what the *Oxford English Dictionary* explains as anything 'acting as a key to some previously undecipherable mystery or unattainable knowledge'.

At least one explanation of the origin of the word *blouse* is that it comes via Latin from the name of the Roman city of Pelusium

---

* Despite popular opinion, the word *Romany* has nothing to do with the Romans, nor Romania for that matter. It actually derives from the Romany word for 'man', *rom*, and so essentially means 'people', or 'humans'.

near Port Said, which was a major fabric-producing centre during the days of the Roman Empire. And the word *ghetto*, another etymological mystery, might derive from an Italian corruption of the Latin name for Egypt, *Aegyptus*.*

Just off the coast of Alexandria is the island of Pharos, which was once home to a great lighthouse considered one of the Seven Wonders of the Ancient World. Although the lighthouse no longer stands (it was demolished in 1480, having been damaged by a series of earthquakes between the tenth and the fourteenth centuries), the name *pharos* eventually became a synonym for a lighthouse or navigational beacon, used in English since the 1550s. And Alexandria itself is the origin of *Alexandrianism*† – a term from literary criticism for an unnecessarily complicated or needlessly obscure word used where a more familiar one would be just as idoneous.‡ It derives from a weighty style of literature and philosophical enquiry, also known as *Alexandrianism*, that developed in Alexandria during the Greek and Roman control of northern Egypt.

The word that brings us to the modern Egyptian capital of Cairo, however, is yet another etymological mystery, and yet another term that has come to be used critically of inappropriately lofty language: *fustian*.

---

* If neither of these two theories are correct, it's possible *blouse* may instead come from a Provençal word, *lano blouso*, literally meaning 'short wool', while *ghetto* could derive from a Venetian word for a foundry, *getto*, as Venice's sixteenth-century ghetto reportedly stood close to a noted metalworks.

† The *alexandrine* – a line of verse comprising twelve syllables – does not take its name from Alexandria, but rather from Alexander the Great. An epic twelfth-century poem retelling the history of Alexander, the *Roman d'Alixandre*, was written in this style and helped popularise it in medieval Europe.

‡ Or 'suitable', if you prefer.

To most people familiar with it, *fustian* is the name of a heavy, thick, woven cotton fabric, often dark in colour and similar in texture to denim. The word first appeared in English in the thirteenth century, when it referred to a specific type of fabric, thinner and coarser than the fustian we know today, made by weaving a cotton weft into a linen warp.

Quite how or why this cotton–linen blend came to be called *fustian* is something of a mystery. One theory claims it might somehow be related to *fustis*, a Latin word for a stick or cudgel (to *fustigate* someone is to club them) but precisely what the connection between the two would be is unclear. A more likely explanation is that the word derives from Fustat, the earliest Muslim capital of Egypt and today one of the ancient suburbs of the city of Cairo. Perhaps it was in Fustat that this fabric was first invented, or else manufactured in great quantities? In the absence of any better explanation, Fustat seems the most likely etymological candidate, but whatever its origin, by the sixteenth century the word *fustian* came to acquire a secondary, and somewhat unexpected, meaning.

Because fustian cloth was often used as lining or padding, in the late 1500s its name came to be used to refer to unnecessarily verbose or overblown language, language characterised by pretentious, high-sounding words and phrases, used merely to 'pad' an otherwise perfectly understandable sentence. Other similar meanings followed, so that before long describing something as *fustian* could also imply that it was invented or entirely nonsensical; earthy or homely; or ranting or bombastic.*

---

* Coincidentally, *bombastic* has a similar history. It derives from *bombast*, a sixteenth-century word for the soft downy head of the cotton plant (which is itself derived from *bombyx*, the Latin name for the silkworm). Because this raw bombast could also be used as padding or wadding, in the late 1500s language it too came to refer to language that was pretentiously inflated, padded out or *bombastic*.

John Milton coined the word *fustianist*, meaning 'a writer of fustian', in 1642, while a verb, *fustianise*, meaning 'to write or use pretentious language', emerged in the early 1800s.

The use of *fustian* to mean 'pompous language' is not as common as it once was, and to most people today the word remains steadfastly attached to the thick fabric it originally described. Either way, it's apparently an ancient suburb of Cairo that we can thank for it.

39

BETHLEHEM, PALESTINE

bedlam

From Egypt we head north into the Holy Land. Our first stop here is Bethlehem, the ancient city outside Jerusalem (and now located in the Palestinian West Bank) known the world over as birthplace of Jesus and site of the ancient Church of the Nativity. Yet the word whose etymology has brought us here now – and the means by which that word appeared in our language – are both about as far removed from the serene cradle of Christianity as it is possible to come. Thanks to several centuries of etymological manoeuvring, the place name *Bethlehem* is the origin of our word *bedlam*.

We might use it to mean 'mayhem' or 'a mad disarray' today, but originally *Bedlam* was simply another name for Bethlehem – an anglicised curtailment that first emerged in the Middle English period as *Bedlem*, or *Bethleem* and even found its way into the Wycliffe Bible in 1382. So it would have remained, were it not for a medieval hospital some two thousand miles away in Bishopsgate, London.

A priory called the New Order of Our Lady of Bethlehem was founded just outside the walls of the City of London in 1247. Originally it was intended merely to be a centre for the collection of alms – funds that were then used to finance the Crusades to the Holy Land – but over the years its purpose, and that of its staff, changed. By the Middle Ages, the priory had become an asylum for the displaced and deranged, and by the time Henry VIII ceded its control to the city in 1547, Bethlehem Hospital, or *Bedlam* as it had become affectionately known, had established itself as one of London's foremost medical institutions, specialising in the treatment of the insane.

References to Bedlam's associations with madness first began to appear in English literature in the mid 1500s. Shakespeare makes references to it in several of his plays:

> *Why, I did no way mistake; this is my king.*
> *What, is he mad? To Bedlam with him!*
> *—Henry IV Part 2* (v.i)

Derivative words and phrases soon followed, so that by the early 1600s to be *bedlam-ripe* was to be fit for the madhouse; a *bedlam-beggar* was a deranged vagrant, or someone who feigned madness to elicit sympathy; to be *bedlam-witted* was to be crazed or senseless; and a *Jack o'Bedlam* or *bedlamite* was an inmate of Bedlam Hospital or, more loosely, a madman or lunatic.

Such was the hospital's reputation that, from expressions such as these, it took only the slightest semantic sidestep to give us the word *bedlam* as it is most often used today. First emerging in the mid 1600s, *bedlam* quickly became a byword for any uproarious scene of deranged disorder or mad confusion.

Of course there's a lot more that the geography of the Holy Land has to offer us here than just a word for madness or derangement: the Israeli city of Jaffa, for instance, is the namesake and origin of the *jaffa* orange. But besides Bethlehem, or rather *Bedlam*, a great number of other place names mentioned in the Bible have fallen into use in English in various allusive and figurative contexts and expressions.

A *Rehoboth*, for instance, is a place of safety or sanctuary, named after the well of Rehoboth in Canaan that, according to the Book of Genesis, was excavated by Isaac. An *Aceldama* is a place of great bloodshed or slaughter, named after the potter's field purchased by Judas using the silver he was paid for betraying Jesus. And as it is said to have been where Jesus walked in anguish before his arrest and crucifixion, *Gethsemane*, outside Jerusalem, has since become a name for any place of mental or spiritual distress.

A *Dead Sea fruit*, or an *apple of Sodom*, is something that does not live up to expectations. Named after the Dead Sea that straddles the Israel–Jordan border – or else the biblical city of Sodom that lay to its north – the legendary fruit was said to look delicious but crumble away to ash and smoke when grasped.

The towns of *Tophet* and *Gehenna* are both singled out in the Book of Jeremiah as the site of ancient human sacrifices, and so have long since been used as bywords for Hell or any place of infernal punishment. The name of *Bethesda*, the site of a pool whose healing waters Jesus used to cure a paralysed man, was used allusively of any place of healing or recovery in nineteenth-century English. And *from Dan to Beersheba* – a phrase repeated several times in the Old Testament, to refer to all the areas settled by the Tribes of Israel – has since become a proverbial expression meaning 'from end to end', or 'from one extreme to another'.

Of all the biblical place names to have found their way into the English language, however, perhaps the most familiar is *Armageddon*. Now merely a synonym for the end of the world, in biblical contexts Armageddon is the name of the final battle between good and evil that will take place the day before Judgement Day. Its name derives from the site at which the battle itself will supposedly take place: *Har Megiddon*, now known as Tel Megiddo, an ancient city atop a shallow hill some twenty miles south of the Israeli city of Haifa.

It's not the only hill in the Holy Land that's ended up in our language . . .

40

MOUNT NEBO, JORDAN

Pisgah

J ust across the border from Israel in Jordan is Mount Nebo, a tall ridge of rock that stands some 2,300 feet above the ancient town of Madaba, roughly midway between the Dead Sea and the Jordanian capital of Amman. Admittedly, you won't find its name, *Nebo*, in the dictionary. Nor, for that matter, will you find it in the Bible. But that's not to say that you won't find it there at all . . .

According to the Bible, having led the exodus from Egypt, Moses guided the Israelites into the wilderness, where they remained for the next forty years. Eventually, they came to the border of Canaan, the land God had promised the Israelites in return for their faith. Following God's instruction, Moses climbed a nearby mountain, named Mount Pisgah, and from there was afforded a glimpse into the Promised Land:

Get thee up into the top of Pisgah, and lift up thine eyes westward, and northward, and southward, and eastward, and behold it with thine eyes: for thou shalt not go over this Jordan. But charge Joshua, and encourage him, and strengthen him: for he shall go over before this people, and he shall cause them to inherit the land which thou shalt see.

—Deuteronomy (3:26–8)

True enough, just as it was explained to him, Moses shortly afterwards perished atop Mount Pisgah, leaving Joshua and the remaining Israelites to travel on to Canaan without him.

It is Moses' Mount Pisgah (a Hebrew name that simply means 'peak') that most Bible scholars today identify as the Jordanian Mount Nebo: its summit provides a panoramic view across the Holy Land, the valley of the River Jordan, and even the cities of Jericho and Jerusalem, and in the early 1900s a Byzantine church commemorating the place of Moses' death was found to have been constructed there in the early fourth century CE. It is through its connection with the Bible's Mount Pisgah that Jordan's Mount Nebo has, albeit indirectly, found its way into our language.

As Moses was merely permitted to see the Promised Land, but not to go there, the name *Pisgah* came to be used in various phrases and expressions to refer to something that remains tantalisingly out of reach. So a *Pisgah sight*, or a *Pisgah view*, is a glimpse of something unobtainable, or a faint view of something that ultimately remains too distant to be obtained, while a *Pisgah hill* is a position or viewpoint that proverbially provides an objective vision of an entire current state of affairs, or else a useful glimpse of the future.

It's the perfect word to mark the halfway point of our journey.

41

SAMARRA, IRAQ

appointment in Samarra

With forty destinations behind us, we pause in Iraq to tell the story behind a little-known expression for a *memento mori* – a reminder of the inevitability of death and that, in the end, we have only one final appointment.

Samarra is a city in central Iraq, just north of Baghdad on the River Tigris. It's also one of the most ancient cities in the world: excavations there have unearthed artefacts dating back to 6000 BCE, and for that reason it was elevated to a World Heritage Site in 2007. But that's not its only claim to fame. Hidden away in the dictionary, the city sits at the heart of an expression, little known unless you're familiar with ancient Mesopotamian fables: *an appointment in Samarra.*

Once upon a time, a merchant in Baghdad sent his servant down to the local market to buy some provisions. The servant duly complied, and headed down to the busy marketplace – where he was promptly jostled to one side by a woman in the crowd.

When he turned around to confront her, the servant saw that this was no ordinary woman who had stepped in his way, but Death, who now stood beside him, her mouth wide open, and her hand raised towards him in a seemingly threatening gesture.

Instantly realising what he had done, the servant panicked and fled the marketplace leaving Death to watch on from the crowd.

Returning to the merchant's shop, the servant explained to his master all about his run-in with Death, and requested to borrow the merchant's horse so that he could ride as far away from Baghdad as he could, as quickly as possible. The merchant agreed, and the servant took the horse from outside the store and rode off. After eighty miles, he arrived in the city of Samarra where, he presumed, Death would never be able to find him.

With his servant now gone, the merchant was left to head down to the marketplace himself – and there, he spotted Death standing contemplatively among the crowd. But rather than flee, the merchant decided to confront Death about the threat she had made that had lost him the services of his servant.

'I am sorry,' Death explained, 'but I did not threaten your servant. I was merely surprised to see him here in Baghdad – because I have an appointment with him tonight in Samarra.'

This fable about the inevitability and inescapability of death was first recorded in the Babylonian Talmud, a collection of local literature compiled in Mesopotamia sometime around the fifth century CE. But if you've heard the expression *an appointment in Samarra* before, then you might be forgiven for thinking this tale was a lot more recent an invention than that.

In his 1933 play, *Sheppey*, the English author and playwright Somerset Maugham had Death tell its own version of this story in the play's closing scene. Inspired by Maugham, the following year the American novelist John O'Hara published his debut novel *Appointment in Samarra* (1934), about the downfall of a wealthy Pennsylvania car dealer. O'Hara included the original quote from Maugham's play in the prologue.

Both these works doubtless helped to popularise the expression *an appointment in Samarra*. But the story that lies behind it is an ancient fable, originating in one of the Middle East's most ancient cities.

42

QUMIS, IRAN

Parthian

We stay in the ancient world for our next story, crossing Iraq's western border into Iran to visit an arid and largely deserted plain not far from the southern shoreline of the Caspian Sea, known locally as Sahr-e Qumis. If a desolate rocky plain doesn't sound like the most exciting destination, it's because, at a rough estimate, we've arrived here at Qumis around two millennia too late.

The history of Qumis, like that of Samarra, dates back into antiquity. Known as Hecatompylos, or 'the city of a hundred gates' to the Greeks, it was visited by Alexander the Great in 330 BCE. Sometime after his death it fell under the control of a local Iranian tribe known as the Parni, who by the end of the third century BCE had taken control both of Qumis itself and of much of the entire ancient state in which it stood.

There, the Parni established a new dynasty, known as the Arascids. They transformed the region into a great and powerful empire, with the city of Qumis established as one of its earliest capitals. This grand Parthian Empire, as it became known, maintained control of the region – even managing to hold its own against the Romans – for the next five centuries, before it finally crumbled in the early 200s CE. Its ancient capital city, Qumis, was finally destroyed by one of history's most devastating earth-quakes in 856. All that remains of the city and its empire today is a barren, rocky plain.

The success of the Parthian Empire in part rested on the tremendous prowess of its armies of cavalrymen. The Parthians' horsemanship was second to none: they were expert riders, both swift and agile, and used their talent to develop an extraordinary array of manoeuvres and tactics that were so skilful they soon became the stuff of legend. One of the most remarkable of these Parthian tactics involved militarising their retreat.

During conflict with an enemy, the Parthians' horsemen would feign a surrender and begin galloping at speed away from the battlefield, seemingly in retreat from their enemy. Buoyed by the prospect of an easy victory, the Parthians' enemies in response would chase after them. But at that point the Parthian cavalrymen would turn in their saddles, while still riding at speed away from the battle, and fire their arrows backwards at their enemy – who now found themselves galloping, at speed, into a devastating shower of arrows and missiles.

This remarkable ploy not only earned the Parthian Empire a place in military history, but also a place in our language. As stories of their retreats became the stuff of legend, the adjective *Parthian* came to be used of battles won in their dying moments, winning decisions made at the eleventh hour, or any actions taken or victories secured at the final opportune time. By the early nineteenth century, the expression *Parthian shot* had emerged to describe a devastatingly cutting comment or knockout blow, delivered in the very final moments of an argument or skirmish. But unfortunately for the ancient Parthians, their place in the language was not to endure.

The fact that their most famous military tactic was enacted in the final moments of conflict – coupled with their name hold-ing a startling similarity to the word *parting* – conspired against them. The original *Parthian shot* quickly became confused with a *parting shot,* and it's the latter of these two that has since become the more commonly used term in the language,* pushing its etymological connection to ancient Parthia out of the spotlight. Not even a last-minute victory could save them now.

---

* Google Ngrams suggests *parting shots* are referenced more than 400 times more frequently in written English today than *Parthian shots.*

43

BUKHARA, UZBEKISTAN

buckram

Our next stop is Bukhara, an ancient city in south Uzbekistan. One of the fifteen fully independent states that emerged from the collapse of the Soviet Union, Uzbekistan now has two notable claims to fame. Firstly, it is one of only two double-landlocked nations in the entire world – that is to say, while Uzbekistan itself is landlocked, all the countries that surround its borders are themselves landlocked too.* Secondly, without Uzbekistan our language would be without a word for a kind of fine linen fabric that, with a little help from William Shakespeare, gave us an eminently useful expression for an absent, invented or wholly non-existent person.

The word that has brought us all the way here to Uzbekistan is *buckram*, the name of a tough, stiff fabric now typically made from cotton, but made originally from woven linen, or even

---

* Those landlocked nations that surround Uzbekistan are Afghanistan, Kazakhstan, Kyrgyzstan, Tajikistan and Turkmenistan. The world's only other double-landlocked nation, incidentally, is Liechtenstein, which is sandwiched between the similarly coastline-less Switzerland and Austria.

horsehair. For that reason the earliest forms of buckram were probably much softer, lighter and more delicate than modern buckram fabric, which is often chemically enhanced or treated with gum to give it a stronger, more hard-wearing finish.

Its name may be relatively unfamiliar today, but the product itself is not. Because of its strength and durability, buckram has long been used to cover cloth-bound books, and for centuries was used to provide a strengthening lining to coats and similar garments.

Etymologically, the origin of the name *buckram* is something of a puzzle. One theory claims that it simply takes its name from the same root as *buck*, meaning 'a male mammal', perhaps referencing that it was once made from woven strands of animal hair. Another claims it might come from an Italian word, *bucherare*, meaning 'to pierce with holes', perhaps a reference to buckram's original mesh-like appearance, while yet another suggests that its roots lie in an old Arabic word, *qiram*, thought to have meant 'veil' or 'shroud'.

There isn't enough etymological evidence to say with any assurance whether any of these theories is accurate or not but perhaps the most likely theory is that *buckram* takes its name from Bukhara.

Another extraordinarily ancient town, Bukhara – and the area around it – has been inhabited for more than five millennia. For many years little more than an isolated town, it flourished in size and significance thanks to its prime location on the Central Asian portion of the Silk Road. As trade with Europe and the Far East blossomed, Bukhara itself flourished, eventually becoming one of the most important Muslim cities in history.

It's thought that it was during this golden age that buckram fabric manufactured in the Uzbek region first began to be imported into Europe – and with it came the name of the city in which it was traded. *Buhkara*, given a little etymological readjustment over the centuries via Latin, Italian and French, eventually morphed into *buckram*, and finally made its debut in written English in the thirteenth century. This particular story, however, doesn't quite end here.

Just as was the case with *fustian*, the various qualities of buckram fabric also came to be employed figuratively. By the sixteenth and seventeenth centuries, the word had come to be used as a synonym for strength or stiffness; for anything or anyone seemingly 'starched' or 'stuck up'; or for anything that gives an appearance of strength, but actually lacks any real substance.

And then, along came Shakespeare:

> *I have peppered two of them. Two I am sure I have paid, two rogues in buckram suits. I tell thee what, Hal, if I tell thee a lie, spit in my face, call me horse. Thou knowest my old ward. Here I lay, and thus I bore my point. Four rogues in buckram let drive at me . . . These four came all afront, and mainly thrust at me. I made me no more ado, but took all their seven points in my target, thus.*
> —*Henry IV Part 1* (II.iv)

In this comic scene in Shakespeare's *Henry IV Part 1*, the swaggering Sir John Falstaff is relating an inflated tale of his own bravery to the young Prince Henry and his companion Ned Poins. But as he continues with his narrative, Falstaff begins to muddle all of the details he has concocted, steadily inflating the number of 'rogues in buckram' with whom he fought from two to four, then to seven, to nine, and eventually eleven. The prince, understandably, is unimpressed: 'These lies are like their father that begets them,' he replies angrily. 'Gross as a mountain.'

Falstaff's buckram-clad rogues might not have actually existed, but a phrase inspired by them certainly does. In use since the 1700s, *men in buckram* has since become a proverbial expression used of someone who does not exist, never existed to begin with, or else is currently (and perhaps permanently, or usually) absent. Often employed in situations where an excuse or alibi is required (or else when a flimsy excuse or alibi needs to be questioned), as the scholar and lexicographer E. C. Brewer put it in his *Dictionary of Phrase and Fable* (1870), *men in buckram* are 'hypothetical men, existing only in the brain of the imaginer'.

44

KABUL, AFGHANISTAN

Afghanistanism

From Bukhara we head due south, over the Hindu Kush and the fringes of the Himalayas, and on to Afghanistan.

At first glance, it might not feel as if there would be much etymological gold to mine in these mountains, but you probably know more Afghan-related words than you might realise. As the name of a type of decorative shawl, for instance, the *afghan* arrived in English in the 1830s. As the name of a type of equally decorative style of carpet, it turned up in the 1870s. The *afghan* hound emerged in the 1880s.* And the fashions of the 1970s left us with an *afghan* sheepskin coat.

But hidden away among the little-used political terms in the dictionary is a much more obscure word that namechecks its home nation of Afghanistan even more blatantly than any of these:

---

* The Afghan hound was originally also known as the *barukhzy*, the name of the Afghan tribe who developed and popularised the breed in its native Afghanistan.

'Afghanistanism' appeals to some editorial writers because they get involved in no local controversies by discussing the sad state of affairs in Afghanistan.
—*Salt Lake Tribune*, 14 June 1954

The journalistic term *Afghanistanism* refers to the preoccupation of some writers, commentators, politicians and the media with events in far-flung locations, at the expense of discussing more contentious or more pressing issues closer to home. But why pick on Afghanistan?

Afghanistan has been in a near-constant state of war and insurgency since the late 1970s, but as the article above proves, the term *Afghanistanism* was in use as far back as the 1950s – while the *Oxford English Dictionary* has recorded the term in use as long ago as 1948. At that time, however, the country was in a period of relative peace and prosperity: despite maintaining a close relationship with the Axis powers of the Second World War, Afghanistan officially remained neutral throughout. In the late 1940s, with both the American and Soviet governments looking to increase their influence on the country, Afghanistan's king, Zahir Shah, accepted financial aid from both sides, and the nation suddenly flourished through the building of new infrastructure, transport links and its first university in modern times. So if you're looking for the 'sad state of affairs' mentioned in the quote above, you might be looking for quite a while.

So why would a word relying on the domestic press's preoccupation with Afghanistan have been coined at a time when Afghanistan itself was in the ascendancy? That, admittedly, is a tough question to answer – and one that has led to suggestions that perhaps here all is not what it seems.

Conceivably, the word *Afghanistanism* was simply coined at random, and the reference to Afghanistan is entirely irrelevant. After all, Afghanistan is the first country in the world alphabetically, so perhaps its name acted as the template for this term for no reason other than that it is a distant country whose name is familiar from the top spot of geographical lists and inventories.

Or perhaps, more plausibly, *Afghanistanism* is a much older word than we have so far been able to prove. Maybe it was coined during the British government's preoccupation with the Anglo-Afghan wars of the late 1800s, or during the Afghan Civil War of 1929? During genuine times of a 'sad state of affairs'?

Until further evidence is forthcoming, we can only speculate. But regardless of its origins, *Afghanistanism* has nevertheless earned its namesake country yet another place in our dictionary.

45

DEOLALI,
INDIA

doolally

We again head south, leaving Afghanistan, crossing Pakistan, and on to India.

One of the largest and most populous countries in Asia, India has long been a major player on the international stage. This, combined with lengthy colonial ties to Great Britain, has seen the country have a considerable impact on the English language: from *avatar* to *yoga*, over the centuries English has adopted a great many words from India's fascinating patchwork of languages.

Bandana, *maharaja*, *guru*, *khaki*, *mantra* and *veranda*, for instance, all derive from Hindi – as does the name of the *cheetah*, which, thanks to its mottled appearance, is probably a distant etymological cousin of another Hindi borrowing, *chintz*.

Thug, *typhoon* and *cummerbund* (which literally means 'waistband') are all Urdu in origin. *Mango*, *teak* and *copra* all come from Malayalam. *Bandicoot* literally means 'pig-rat' in Telugu. The original hot *toddy* was a Marathi word, *tadi*, for a kind of palm wine. And that glass of *punch* you had at your last office party takes its name from the Sanskrit word for 'five', *panca* – a reference to the drink's original five ingredients: usually milk, curd, clarified butter, honey and sugar.

When it comes to words derived from Indian place names, we're still spoilt for choice; there's certainly a lot more to talk about here than just *Darjeeling* tea.

Calico cloth, for instance, takes its name from the Malabar port of Calicut, now Kozhikode, where European explorers first encountered it. The original *dungarees* were made from a coarser type of calico known as *dungri*, which in turn took its name from the suburb of Mumbai where it was made. A rider's traditional *jodhpur* trousers take their name from the town of Jodhpur in Rajasthan. *Dum-dum* bullets, specialised projectiles manufactured with an exposed soft core that expands on impact, acquire their name from the town of Dum-Dum near Kolkata, which was once the site of a major local arsenal. And while the entire state of Bengal is namechecked in the origin of the *bungalow* (which literally means 'Bengal-style house'), all of India lies at the etymological roots of both *indigo* dye (derived from a Greek word meaning 'Indian') and the *tamarind* (literally the 'date of India').

But we've not come all this way to talk about any of those. Instead, we're here for an idiosyncratic and quintessentially British-sounding word for madness or muddle-headedness, whose story begins at a town not far inland from India's west coast.

In 1861, a British military cantonment was established in Deolali, a small town in Maharashtra state, around a hundred miles east of Mumbai. British troops arriving in India would be taken to this camp to train and acclimatise, while 'time-expired' troops whose service was now complete would make the opposite journey, embarking from Deolali for Mumbai, before taking the long trip home to Blighty.*

---

* As a slang name for England or Great Britain, *Blighty* too has Indian origins. It derives from an Urdu word, *vilayati*, that literally means 'foreign', but was used by Urdu speakers in the nineteenth century for British

When the camp first opened in the mid nineteenth century, this exchange of personnel took place only during the winter and spring months, October to March, as the scorching summer heat and monsoons of early autumn made year-round transportation all but impossible. Places on the ships home were ultimately filled during the intervening months – but that meant that any soldier unfortunate enough to end his tour of duty in the spring would often have to wait until the end of the year to catch the first transport ship home. And for some, that long wait proved too much to bear.

Conditions in the camp were poor. Equipment was scarce, beds were infested with fleas, and the air was thick with mosquitoes. Malarial infections were common, but so too were grim venereal diseases spread via brothels in the surrounding towns and cities that were too close for some recruits to resist. Deolali ultimately established itself partly as military transit camp, and partly as military hospital. But all these factors together – combined with the unfamiliar culture, oppressive heat and sheer boredom of the long wait for repatriation – conspired to make it an uncomfortable and distressing place. Suicide rates among troops waiting to be sent home were high, while many other recruits spiralled into madness as they struggled to deal with the psychological aftermath of their military service and the dreadful conditions.

The camp's association with both madness and mind-breaking boredom soon established itself in the minds of the nineteenth-century military. Its name, *Deolali*, became a synonym for the madness or derangement associated with it, while an invented disease, *Deolali tap* ('tap' being a local word for a fever), became a catch-all name for the psychological conditions that plagued the troops awaiting their transport home:

or European people in particular. At its root is an Urdu word meaning 'country' or 'dominion', *vilayet*, which is itself of Arabic origin.

Time-expired men sent to Deolalie from their different units might have to wait for months before a troop-ship fetched them home ... [They] had no arms or equipment; they showed kit now and then and occasionally went on a route-march, but time hung heavily on their hands ... The well-known saying among soldiers when speaking of a man who does queer things, 'Oh, he's got the Doo-lally tap,' originated I think in the peculiar way men behaved owing to the boredom of that camp.
—Frank Richards, *Old Soldier Sahib* (1936)

Doolally, a quirky anglicised form of *Deolali*, emerged in the early 1900s. Gradually, from its original associations with madness and insanity, its meaning became considerably looser and less serious over time, so that by the 1950s *doolally* was being used as another word for 'eccentric', 'confused' and even 'drunk', as well as 'mad' or 'crazed'. But to most English speakers today it remains most closely associated with madness, and in particular a temporary state of madness or period of crazed, peculiar behaviour, seen in someone who is otherwise perfectly level-headed.

46

COLOMBO, SRI LANKA

serendipity

From the Indian mainland, we cross to the island of Sri Lanka, just off the southernmost tip of Central Asia.

Sri Lanka is roughly the same size as Scotland, but is home to more than four times as many people, the majority of whom speak either the Sinhalese or the Tamil language. Neither of these has contributed a great many words to the English dictionary: Sinhalese is probably best known as the origin of *beriberi*,* while the most familiar Tamil words used in English are probably *cheroot*, and *catamaran*, a double-hulled boat whose name literally means 'tied wood'. Besides these, a list of Sri Lankan words borrowed in English would drift into ever more obscure territory, with entries like *patana* (a forested upland slope); *ratemahatmaya* (a local Sri Lankan chieftain†); *kabaragoya* (a species of water monitor); and *tic-polonga* (a local name for the Russell's viper).

---

* *Beri* is a Sinhalese word meaning 'weakness', or 'lack of strength'; duplicating it here serves to intensify its meaning, so *beriberi* could be said to mean 'great weakness'.

† Literally, 'gentleman of the country' in Sinhalese.

The languages of Sri Lanka might not be the most fruitful source of English words but the island itself is a different story. Thanks to the unlikely sounding combination of an eighteenth-century English author and politician and the island's Arabic name, Sri Lanka is the origin of one word with which you will undoubtedly be familiar.

The English politician in question here is Horace Walpole. A son of Sir Robert Walpole, the first prime minister of Great Britain, Horace served in the British parliament for almost thirty years, from 1741 to 1768, during which time he also found time to publish what is generally regarded as the first Gothic novel, *The Castle of Otranto* (1764). But that wasn't his only contribution to literature.

On 28 January 1754, Walpole wrote a letter to his friend (and distant cousin) Sir Horace Mann, who at the time was serving as a British diplomatic envoy in Florence. Mann had recently mailed to Walpole a much prized painting of Bianca Cappello, an Italian noblewoman who had married into the Medici dynasty in the sixteenth century, and while waiting for the picture to arrive Walpole had by chance stumbled across the Cappello coat of arms in an old book on heraldry. 'This discovery, indeed,' he wrote, 'is almost of that kind which I call Serendipity.'

That word, *serendipity*, was seemingly Walpole's own invention: no record of it has been unearthed any earlier than this letter. But that's not to say that he had made the word up out of thin air. As he continued to explain:

Serendipity [is] a very expressive word . . . you will understand it better by the derivation than by the definition. I once read a silly fairy tale, called 'The Three Princes of Serendip'; as their Highnesses travelled, they were always making discoveries, by accidents and sagacity, of things which they were not in quest of: for instance, one of them discovered that a mule blind of the right eye had travelled the same road lately, because the grass was eaten only on the left side, where it was worse than on the right – now do you understand Serendipity?

An anecdote about a half-blind mule is hardly the most straight-forward definition of *serendipity*, but Walpole's example of what he called 'accidental sagacity' nevertheless matches what we would call a *serendipitous* discovery today. It's the title of the 'silly fairy tale' he alludes to, however, that is the origin of the word itself.

Serendip is an old name for Sri Lanka, thought to derive via Arabic from an ancient Sanskrit word meaning 'dwelling-place of lions'. Walpole's 'Princes of Serendip', ultimately, were Sri Lanka princes, and it's from their island home that he coined the word we still use for a happy accident today.

But if that's a happy accident, what might we call the exact opposite? Well, for that, we can turn to the English writer William Boyd, who coined the antonym *zemblanity* in his 1998 novel *Armadillo*. Describing it as the practice of 'making unhappy, unlucky and expected discoveries by design', Boyd took the word *zemblanity* from Novaya Zemlya, the name of a bleak and barren Arctic archipelago in the far north of Russia that was once used as a Soviet nuclear testing site – about as far removed from a tropical island as it's possible to be.

47

SAMUT SONGKHRAM, THAILAND

Siamese twins

Leaving Sri Lanka, we head back to the Asian mainland, travelling more than fifteen hundred miles across the Bay of Bengal to Thailand.

Our destination is Samut Songkhram, a town some forty miles from Bangkok. There, on 11 May 1811, twin brothers Chang and Eng Bunker were born. Given that Thailand was still officially known as Siam at the time, and given that Chang and Eng were born conjoined, attached by a strip of cartilage at their chests, the pair were the original *Siamese twins*.*

But how did the brothers come to be known enough outside their native Thailand to inspire a term that has endured in the language for two centuries? Well, to say that the brothers lived an extraordinary life is something of an understatement.

---

* As Chang and Eng's parents were of Chinese descent, in their native Siam the brothers were known as the 'Chinese twins'.

According to legend, on their birth the king of Siam, Rama II, thought their appearance a bad omen and demanded they be killed; fortunately, the sentence was never carried out. Their father and five siblings all died in a cholera epidemic in 1819, after which they were raised single-handedly by their mother. At the age of fourteen, having now become national icons, they were sent by the king to Cochin-China on a diplomatic mission, accompanied by a hundred Siamese armed guards to protect them from the attention of ogling crowds en route. But, in 1824, that did not stop them from attracting the attention of a Scottish merchant working in Siam, named Robert Hunter.

Hunter saw potential in exhibiting Chang and Eng* as a curiosity, and spent several years arranging a deal with the brothers, their mother and the Siamese authorities. Finally, when they were eighteen years old, the deal was finalised: the brothers were to be paid $10 per day (a salary eventually increased fivefold when they proved a success), while their mother was to be paid a one-off sum of $3,000 (of which, reportedly, she only ever received around $500). They departed Siam in April 1829, and arrived in Boston the following August, where they were exhibited to the paying public for the very first time. They proved an instant sensation.

Managed by Hunter's business partner, Abel Coffin, the brothers were promoted as 'The Siamese Double Boys', and over the next decade were exhibited under that name to packed

---

* A popular etymological legend claims the brothers' names mean 'left' and 'right'. Despite being untrue, the myth nevertheless inspired a poem by the American journalist and writer William Linn Keese:

> *Their names grew out of a family hitch,*
> *How best to label t'other from which;*
> *And we gather from this domestic plight*
> *That Chang meant 'left' and Eng meant 'right'.*
> —William Linn Keese, 'The Siamese Twins' (1902)

houses across America and Europe. The success of their tour doubtless helped to establish the term *Siamese* in the language as a synonym for 'conjoined': it had fallen into broader use in the language as early as the 1830s,* and the brothers were soon established as a metaphor for anything or anyone inseparable from anything or anyone else:

> *People who have been inseparable and found all their happiness in each other for five years are in a sort of Siamese-twin condition, that other people are not likely to regard with tolerance or even with belief.*
> —George Eliot, Letter to Charles Bray (1859)

As for the brothers themselves, in 1839 they settled in America and married two sisters, Adelaide and Sarah-Anne Yates, and fathered twenty-one children between them. Alas, financial problems compelled the brothers to return to show business after the Civil War, and in 1868 they accepted an invitation from showman P. T. Barnum to once more take their tour to Europe.

---

* Proving just how quickly Chang and Eng established themselves as a sensation, a verb *Siamese* – defined by the *Oxford English Dictionary* as 'to join, unite, or couple, after the manner of the Siamese twins' – was first used in an edition of *Fraser's Magazine* in May 1830, just nine months after the brothers arrived in America. In a discussion of a new divorce bill recently debated in the House of Commons, the magazine lamented:

> *The instant the smiling pair leave the church, and the blushing bride hangs on the arm of her simpering swain, they become one with such intensity, that you might as well try to hew adamant with a straw as effect a separation. They are dovetailed into an unfrangible integer – Siamesed by a cord which defies the knife of the most skilful surgeon that ever shred limbs in an hospital.*

Tragically, just two years later, Chang suffered a stroke from which he never recovered, and in 1874 Eng awoke one morning to find that his brother had died during the night. Within three hours, Eng too had passed away.

With a life story as remarkable as that, it's easy to see how Chang and Eng helped to establish the word *Siamese* across the English-speaking world.

48

PHNOM PENH, CAMBODIA

gamboge

From Thailand we cross the border into Cambodia, for the quick story behind the name of a rich orange-yellow colour: *gamboge*.

To English speakers today, *gamboge* is probably best known as the name of the saffron-like colour of Buddhist monks' robes but, according to Herman Melville, it was the colour of London's smog at the height of the Industrial Revolution:

> *Upon sallying out this morning, encountered the old-fashioned pea soup London fog – of a gamboge color. It was lifted, however, from the ground & floated in mid-air. When lower, it is worse.*
> —Herman Melville, *Journal of a Visit to London and the Continent* (1849)

The colour takes its name from an artist's pigment and dye, which has been known as *gamboge* since the seventeenth century. The pigment in turn acquired its name from the *gamboge* tree, from which it is ultimately manufactured. And the *gamboge* tree takes *its* name from the raw product extracted from it – a thick, milky gum known as *gamboge* resin, or *gambogium* – which has long been used to make the pigment (and a mild purgative medicine, should you ever need it).

But where did the name *gamboge* itself come from?

The trees that produce gamboge are all native to southeast Asia, in particular to the nations of Thailand and neighbouring Cambodia. It was from there that *gambogium* resin was first imported into Europe in the 1600s, and, simply enough, the resin took its name from the Latin name for Cambodia, *Gambogia*. All in all, it's one of those etymological connections that seems obvious only once you know to look for it.

49

SHANGHAI, CHINA

Shanghaiing

L eaving Cambodia, we cross Vietnam and the South
China Sea and land seventeen hundred miles away in
Shanghai, the largest city in China – and one of a hand-
ful of contenders for the title of largest city in the world.

Given how significant a location it is, it's perhaps unsurpris-
ing that Shanghai has found itself in the dictionary on more than
one occasion. In Australian slang, for instance, a *shanghai* is a
catapult or slingshot. To darts players, *Shanghai* is the name of a
variant of the game in which players, armed with three darts at
a time, must hit each number on the board in numerical order
– with any failure to score in each round leading to immediate
elimination from the game.*

But both these meanings apparently derive from an even
earlier use of the place name as a verb: since the early 1900s,

---

* Another version of these rules has each player given a number, which
they must first score before attempting to hit other players' numbers, and
thereby eliminate them from the game. Regardless of the rules, in either
version it is the sense of being unceremoniously ejected from the game
that is the reasoning behind the name *Shanghai*.

Shanghai has been used to mean 'to force or constrain someone to do something against their will'. And this meaning in turn derives from an even earlier use of the name *Shanghai* from late-nineteenth-century nautical slang – when it referred to an even more specific, and even more nefarious, practice:

> *I got something to eat, and what I supposed was some coffee, but I had hardly drunk it when a stupor seized me, from which I only recovered under . . . a bucket or two of water, which was soused over me. Then I found myself . . . on board the ship Belvedere . . . bound for Liverpool . . . where we were to land sixty thousand bricks, and reload with cotton. We were told that we had shipped, and had received eighty dollars each in advance. Protest was useless, and we obeyed when we were ordered to man the windlass quickly under penalty of having our heads smashed. This was Wednesday. We could give no account of ourselves since Monday . . . To be carried or forced on board of a ship in this manner is what is termed in sailor parlance being 'Shanghaied'.*
> —Samuel Samuels, *From the Forecastle to the Cabin* (1887)

Originally, to be *shanghaied* was to be drugged (or 'otherwise rendered insensible', according to the *Oxford English Dictionary*) and drafted against your will onto the crew of a vessel short of hands. Typically, by the time the unfortunate victim of the *shanghaiing* regained consciousness, the ship onto which he had been conscripted had already left port and had entered the open ocean; escape from your *shanghaiing* was all but impossible.

But why namecheck China's largest city for quite such an ugly practice? It's all too tempting to think the worst here: namely that disreputable sea captains in the coastal cities of China must once have been frequent users of this ploy, and that unsolicited enrolments onto ships in Shanghai must once have been a common problem in the city. In fact, it seems quite the opposite is true.

During a time of ever escalating maritime trade with the Far East in the late 1800s, the port city of Shanghai was merely among the most frequent destinations for ships leaving ports in Europe and America. Those crew members who were unscrupulously drafted onto the ships' crews found themselves in Shanghai more often than anywhere else *at the end* of their nightmare journeys, having been drugged or set upon elsewhere at the start of their ordeal. (In Samuel Samuels' account above, for instance, he was drugged in a Baltimore boarding house.)

So it might not have been Shanghai where this tactic was most used, but it was certainly where the fruits of its labour often ended up. And that alone was certainly enough to earn the city its permanent – if not entirely welcome – place in our language.

50

SHANGDU, CHINA

Xanadu

Of course, *Shanghaiing* sailors isn't the only word in our language that can trace its origins back to the Chinese map. The thin cotton fabric known as *nankeen* takes its name from the city of Nanjing, for instance. *Lhasa apso* dogs namecheck the Tibetan capital of Lhasa, where the breed was originally developed.* *Macau*, a former Portuguese colony known for its gambling, is also the name of a card game similar to baccarat, but played only one card at a time. *Kaolin*, or 'China clay', one of the raw ingredients of porcelain, is named after the Chinese village of Gaoling where it was once produced. And indeed China was once so well known for the production of porcelain that the entire country's name became a synonym for any porcelain-ware or pottery in the sixteenth century.

From Shanghai we head more than eight hundred miles north to a city whose contribution to our language – with a little help from Samuel Taylor Coleridge – is a word for a place of stunning beauty, luxury or serenity.

---

* *Apso* means 'bearded', or 'woolly', in Tibetan.

The city in question is Shangdu, the ancient Mongol city founded by Kublai Khan, a grandson of Genghis Khan, in the thirteenth century. In 1272, Khan made the city of Dadu (modern-day Beijing) the capital of his Yuan dynasty, while the city of Shangdu in Inner Mongolia, two hundred miles north of Beijing, became his summer capital.

Shangdu was a grand walled city, roughly square in shape, in the centre of which stood Kublai Khan's summer palace. Marco Polo is known to have visited the city in 1275, where he found 'a very fine marble palace' at the centre of a vast walled compound, 'the rooms of which are all gilt and painted with figures of men and beasts and birds . . . all executed with such exquisite art that you regard them with delight and astonishment'. In its palace grounds were vast expanses of 'fountains and rivers and brooks and beautiful meadows', where a menagerie of 'all kinds of wild animals excluding such as are of ferocious nature' roam free. Khan, he explained, spent the three summer months of June, July and August in this city, before returning to the southern capital when the fierce heat of the summer began to cool.

Marco Polo's description, along with several other notable accounts like it written over the centuries that followed, helped to establish an almost mythical image of the city of Shangdu in European minds. In 1797, one of these accounts – by the English clergyman Samuel Purchas – fell into the hands of the poet Samuel Taylor Coleridge.

According to his own account, Coleridge was reading Purchas's description of the city of Shangdu when he happened to fall asleep, with the last words he remembered reading being:

Here the Khan Kubla commanded a palace to be built, and a stately garden thereunto. And thus ten miles of fertile ground were inclosed with a wall.
—Samuel Purchas, *Purchas His Pilgrimes* (1625)

Coleridge was unwell at the time, and medicating his illness with opium. As he slept, the opium fuelled an extraordinarily vivid dream, in which he imagined seeing Shangdu – known at the time as Xanadu – in all its glory. When he awoke, Coleridge grabbed his pen, paper and ink, and composed the following lines:

In Xanadu did Kubla Khan
A stately pleasure-dome decree:
Where Alph, the sacred river, ran
Through caverns measureless to man
Down to a sunless sea.

Coleridge's poem, 'Kubla Khan' (1797), proved immensely popular on its publication in 1816, and the name *Xanadu* soon caught the public imagination. Before long, based on Coleridge's description, its name was being used figuratively in English, as a byword for any place of epic grandeur, extravagance or serenity.

As for the actual city of Shangdu that inspired it, it fell to the Ming Army in the fourteenth century, and as the last of the Khan dynasty fled the city, it was razed to the ground by Zhu Yuanzhang, the founder of China's Ming dynasty. Today, only ruins remain of a city once grand enough to earn a place in our language that has endured for almost eight hundred years.

51

KAGOSHIMA, JAPAN

satsuma

We now head more than a thousand miles south-east across the Yellow Sea to Japan, where we could have picked any one of a number of places, from the city of Akita, two hundred and fifty miles north of Tokyo, where *akita* dogs were first bred, to Kobe, near Osaka, the namesake of world-renowned *Kobe* beef. Even the name *Japan* itself has fallen into use in English, both as the name of an especially hard black varnish that originated there, and as a verb meaning 'to lacquer' or 'to cover with black gloss'.* But the place we're interested in is the city of Kagoshima, capital of the Kagoshima region of Japan that occupies the southernmost tip of the southernmost island, Kyushu, of the four main islands of Japan.

The word we owe to the region around Kagoshima has its origins back on the Asian mainland. Mandarin orange trees, thought to have originated around the city of Wenzhou† in

---

* Or, in eighteenth-century slang at least, 'to ordain as a cleric' – a reference to the 'black coat' that japanned wood is covered in.
† At the time, Wenzhou was known as Unsyu, a name that is still reflected in the fruit's Latin name, *Citrus unshiu*.

eastern China, were brought to Japan more than seven hundred years ago, where they soon thrived in Kyushu's warm, subtropical climate and fertile volcanic soil. The fruit these trees produced – known as the *mikan* in its native Japanese – were seedless, smaller and squatter in shape than the ordinary mandarin orange, had softer flesh, and a sweeter, more delicate flavour. As a result they quickly proved popular both in Japan and, from the late eighteenth century onwards at least, overseas.

In the late 1700s, some early cultivars of these Japanese *mikan* orange trees are believed to have been introduced to the United States by Jesuit missionaries who had served in Japan. Groves were planted at various locations across the southern states, and quickly thrived – but it would be another century before the fruit they produced caught on nationwide.

Ann van Valkenburgh, the wife of Robert van Valkenburgh, a former US diplomatic minister resident to Japan, is popularly credited with reintroducing these oranges to Florida in the late 1870s. Presumably unaware that the fruits had already arrived in the US sometime earlier, Ann renamed them after the district of Kagoshima in which she knew they had originated back in Japan: the newly rechristened *satsuma* orange had finally arrived in the West.*

By this point the satsuma's geographical namesake had vanished from the map: in 1871, a nationwide reorganisation of the feudal provinces of Japan had seen the ancient province of Satsuma incorporated into a newly formed prefecture, named after the region's largest city, Kagoshima. Nevertheless the name *satsuma* remained in use in America, where by the early 1910s

---

* The Satsuma Province of Kyushu is also the origin of Satsuma-ware pottery, an especially fine and highly decorated porcelain that became popular in the United States in the 1870s. Its immense popularity at the time undoubtedly helped to reinforce *satsuma* as the orange's name of choice the following decade.

more than a million of these Satsuma orange trees had been imported and planted; the belt of orangeries that now began to thrive across the southeast USA were mirrored in a string of newly founded towns named 'Satsuma' that sprang up in Florida, Alabama, Louisiana and Texas. Still today, the satsuma remains one of the most popular varieties of orange on the market, even though its geographical connection to Japan has long since disappeared.

52

MANILA, PHILIPPINES

Manila paper

The seven thousand islands of the Philippines, thirteen hundred miles southwest of Japan, provide the origin of a word that has fallen into fairly frequent use in the English language, attached to a product that has become all but ubiquitous in modern life.

No, the product in question here is not *paribuntal*, the criminally neglected name of a type of fine straw used to make straw hats, which takes its name from the northern Filipino town of Paracale. Nor is it the *batangas* knife, a type of fold-ing dual-bladed pocketknife originating in Batangas, a province on the largest of the Philippines' islands, Luzon. Instead, we've landed here in the Filipino capital for the story behind *manila* paper.

If you've ever worked in an office or received a bill through the mail (which, let's face it, covers pretty much everybody) then you'll have handled *manila* paper – the rough, relatively inexpensive, buff-coloured paper that's typically used to make envelopes and packaging. Manila paper's distinctive colour and texture (and for that matter, its name) all derive from so-called Manila hemp, a plant, also known as *abacá*, that is native to the

Philippines' islands.* Unlike traditional papermaking, which uses pressed wood pulp, manila paper is made from the abacá plant's tough outer-stem fibres, which are among the strongest naturally occurring fibres in the world. As well as paper, in its native Philippines abacá is used to make twine, matting and even rope.

Papermaking techniques were probably brought to the Philippines from China in antiquity, but manila paper did not earn its ubiquitous spot in every in-tray the world over until the nineteenth century, when paper made from Manila hemp first began to be manufactured in the United States. It's thought that the earliest American manila paper was made from recycled or disused hemp ropes, which at the time would have offered a cheaper and more readily available alternative to other papermaking materials, such as wood and linen. These fibres were then crushed and pulped using a less refined method than is used to make ordinary white paper, which left manila paper with a rougher texture, and many of its constituent fibres still clearly visible.

That rougher texture, however, made manila paper the perfect hard-wearing alternative to white paper, and consequently it soon caught on for use in the likes of envelopes and protective document folders. According to papermaking legend, the original manila folder – made from a single sheet of manila paper folded in two – was invented in haste during the American Civil War, when precious maps, records and similar documents had to be stored and carried to and from the battlefield.

By the 1860s manila paper was well enough known to make its first recorded appearances in stationers' catalogues, with the earliest specific reference to a *manila envelope* following on in 1889. And your in-tray (or, if you're more organised, your out-tray) has been full of them ever since.

---

* Despite the name, *abacá* isn't actually a species of hemp at all but a member of the banana family. The name Manila hemp refers to the fact that it was used and farmed like hemp for its fibres.

53

MAKASSAR, INDONESIA

antimacassar

From the Philippines, we travel almost due south to Indonesia, heading for a port on the central island of Sulawesi, at the eastern end of the Java Sea.

Java itself is probably the most familiar word we owe to Indonesia: coffee grown and imported from the island of Java was first described in English in the mid eighteenth century, and has proved so popular over the centuries since that its name, *java*, has been used as a jargonish nickname for coffee generally since the mid 1800s. (And *java patrol* has been truckers' slang for a coffee break since the 1940s.)

Also from Indonesia, *bantam* hens take their name from the seaport of Banten in western Java. Unlike the *turkey* vs *Turkey* problem that we encountered earlier in our journey, *bantams* did indeed originate in and around Banten: European travellers and traders in southeast Asia looking to restock their ships' provisions before making the long journey home found the smaller-than-normal hens sold in the markets of Banten made a useful and easily kept source of fresh meat and eggs. Ultimately, the name of the port at which they were purchased passed on to the birds themselves. *Bantamweight* boxers, meanwhile – so called as they're among the lightest professional fighters, weighing between 115 and 118lbs – have been fighting among themselves since the 1880s.

Another seaport on our journey is Makassar, the largest city and provincial capital of the island Sulawesi, which lies almost perfectly central in the Indonesian archipelago. An etymological curiosity, its name came to be attached to a product that originated there but ended up enduring in the language as something designed to keep that same product at bay. During the Dutch control of Indonesia in the nineteenth century, Makassar established itself as a major trade port through which many of the commodities produced in the eastern islands of the country could be exported – including pearls, rattan, teak, sandalwood and the raw ingredients of what would become known as *Rowland's Macassar Oil.*

Alexander Rowland was an eighteenth-century London barber, who in the early 1780s began marketing his own brand of haircare oil made from a coconut or palm oil, imported from Makassar, mixed with a variety of other fragrant oils and colourants. From his barber's shop in St James Street, London, Rowland began selling his so-called 'Macassar oil' as a treatment for men's hair. According to advertisements, the oil claimed to strengthen and smooth the hair, while accelerating its growth and slickly holding whatever style the wearer wanted in place.

Within two decades, Macassar oil had become the go-to product for the capital's most style-conscious gentlemen, and Rowland's product had become so successful that the A. Rowland & Sons Company was formed to deal with the demand. But as the use of Macassar oil became ever more widespread, an unusual problem began to plague the nation . . .

Because the oil did not dry like gels and other hair treatments do, the raw ingredients of Macassar oil were very easily transferred onto other surfaces – most notably headrests, cushions and the upholstered backs of chairs. To get around this problem, in

1852 the 'anti-macassar' was invented: a decorative, and often crocheted, detachable fabric covering that could be placed over the backs of chairs and headrests to protect them from the hair products of the gentlemen sitting in them. The *antimacassar* proved so popular that long after Macassar oil treatments fell out of fashion in the 1900s the word remained in place in the language for any similar item that was often now used – with the oily-haired problems of the past thankfully now gone – purely for decoration.

54

TASMANIA, AUSTRALIA

vandemonianism

As the water opens up ahead of us, and the landmasses grow fewer and further between, the distances between our destinations become ever longer. From Sulawesi in the north, we take a three-thousand-mile trip south across mainland Australia and down to Tasmania.

Many of the nations on our travels have contributed only a single word or two to our language. But in Australia – itself an English-speaking country, with long colonial ties to Britain – we're once more spoilt for etymological choice.

The town of Murrumbidgee in New South Wales, for example, is the origin of the expression *Murrumbidgee whaler*, a nineteenth-century nickname for an idler or slow worker. It derives from the local swagmen in the area, who would earn a living during only part of the year, selling fish caught using a hook and a length of twine:

> *Murrumbidgee whalers are a class of loafers who work for about six months in the year – i.e. during shearing and harvest – and camp the rest of the time in bends of rivers, and live by fishing and begging.*
> —G. H. 'Ironbark' Gibson, *Southerly Busters* (1878)

Also from New South Wales, the *sydharb* is a unit of capacity – often used to quantify the likes of floodwaters or reservoirs – equal to 500 billion litres, or the approximate volume of Sydney Harbour. And named after the address of the Supreme Court in Sydney, *to go up King Street* was a nineteenth-century euphemism for going bankrupt – the Australian version of London's *on Carey Street*.

The *peach melba* dessert famously takes its name from the acclaimed opera singer Dame Nellie Melba, but less well known is the fact that Dame Nellie in turn took her stage name from her place of birth: she was born Helen Porter Mitchell, in Melbourne – aka 'Melba' – in 1861.

A *Queensland sore* is a festering, poorly healing sore, once considered symptomatic of scurvy – a disease that required fresh fruit and vegetables, difficult to track down in the Australian outback, to remedy. The Queensland town of Moreton Bay became so known for the quality of its fig trees in the mid nineteenth century that *Moreton Bay fig* fell into use in Australian rhyming slang for a 'fizgig' – a sixteenth-century word that came to be used in criminal lingo for a police informant. All that had changed by the 1950s, however, as by then a *Moreton Bay* had morphed from an untrustworthy accomplice into a byword for a gullible fool, or the victim of a confidence trick.

As much as it might sound like a cheap pun, the so-called *Coolgardie safe* – a rudimentary device for keeping food cold in hot climates – was invented in the tiny isolated gold-rush town of Coolgardie, three hundred and fifty miles east of Perth, in the late 1890s. Little more than a miniature cupboard with water-soaked mesh or hessian for its door and sides, the *Coolgardie* kept the local prospectors' food cool and guarded against insects in the fierce heat of the Australian outback.

While we're in the outback, *Min-Min lights* are an eerie and unexplained phosphorescence that is said to follow lonely travellers around the remote Queensland desert. If not a word derived from some native Aboriginal language, the name *Min-Min* could simply derive from that of a hotel in the outback town of Boulia where the lights were first reported – though whether the lights or the hotel were named first is a mystery as difficult to solve as the lights themselves.

And the name of Tasmania's River Derwent, on the banks of which was a notorious prison settlement, is the origin of an old nineteenth-century word, *derwenter*, for a released convict. But it's another altogether more impressive-sounding word associated with Tasmania's criminal past that concerns us now.

Beginning in the 1780s, Britain began using its recently acquired territories in Australia as the site of penal colonies, to which convicts – found guilty of anything from theft to bigamy* – would be sent, often for years at a time. The first of these correctional colonies was established in New South Wales, but as they became full other sites began to be considered. In 1803, an expedition was sent to Tasmania to investigate the possibility of housing convicts offshore, and the following year a station was established at what would eventually grow to become the island's capital, Hobart.

The transportation of convicts to New South Wales came to an end in the 1840s, after which the number of convicts being sent to Tasmania increased immensely; by the 1850s, the island was one of only a handful of penal colonies that remained active in the British Empire. This quickly established an association

---

* All theft above the value of one shilling was at one point potentially punishable by transportation – as were such bizarre offences as carrying too many paying passengers in a riverboat, stealing another person's post, burning clothes and uprooting trees. Transportation to the other side of the world might sound like an impossibly harsh sentence for such relatively petty crimes, but at a time when capital punishment was still retained for more serious crimes such as rape and murder, transportation was perceived as a more lenient, yet still punitive, punishment.

with all things criminal in Tasmania – a reputation that proved difficult to shift.

At the time, Tasmania wasn't known as 'Tasmania', but rather as Van Diemen's Land – a name bestowed on it by the Dutch explorer Abel Tasman, the first European to set foot on the island (and its eventual namesake). Tasman named the island in honour of his financial patron Anthony van Diemen, the Governor-General of the Dutch East Indies, who in 1642 funded Tasman's voyage around the Indian and western Pacific Oceans, during which the island was discovered.

Etymologically, that explains why a *Vandemonian* is an old-fashioned name for someone from Tasmania. Combined with Van Diemen's Land's long-standing association with criminality, it also explains the origin of the curious word *vandemonianism*:

> *Mr. Houston looked upon the conduct of hon. gentlemen opposite as ranging from the extreme of vandemonianism to the extreme of namby-pambyism.*
> —*Hansard* (1863)

According to *Austral English: A Dictionary of Australasian Words* (1898), *vandemonianism* is 'rowdy conduct, like that of an escaped convict'; the change in the spelling of *Diemen* in the centre of the word is, according to another nineteenth-century dictionary of *Slang and its Analogues Past and Present* (1890), intended as 'a glance at "demon".'

Happily for the people of Tasmania (and, we can presume, the entirely innocent Anthony van Diemen), the word *vandemonianism* does not seem to have endured. After penal transportation fell out of favour in the British justice system in the late 1860s, the island's association with crime and criminality dwindled. And after the name *Tasmania* was adopted in 1856, use of the word *vandemonianism* and its derivatives likewise vanished from the language.

55

KARITANE, NEW ZEALAND

Karitane

Twelve hundred miles across the Tasman Sea from Tasmania is the coastal town of Karitane, on South Island, New Zealand. Established as a whaling station in the early 1800s, Karitane (pronounced 'ka-ruh-*tahn-ee*') is home to barely three hundred people. Nevertheless, at least one of the tiny town's past residents achieved a level of fame and success that not only altered medical practice in his native New Zealand, but landed his unassuming home a place in the dictionary.

Truby King was born in New Plymouth, on New Zealand's North Island, in 1858. Having studied medicine in Europe – where he also met his wife, Isabella – King returned home to New Zealand in the late 1880s to begin his practice. Although his areas of expertise ranged from surgery to veterinary medicine, he initially focused on psychiatry and the treatment of mental health conditions, and in 1889 took the prestigious position of medical superintendent at an asylum in Seacliff, near Dunedin, on South Island. There, he took to implementing many of his own theories and treatments, advocating the importance of exercise, recreation and, above all, a nutritious diet in maintaining long-lasting mental and physical health.

It was while working at Seacliff that in 1905 the Kings adopted a baby girl, Mary, whose mother had found herself unable to raise the child single-handedly after the sudden death of her young daughter's father. Isabella became concerned that the girl was not developing as healthily and as robustly as she could, and put the issue of Mary's health to her husband. Before long, Truby had put all of his exceptional experience and nutritional knowledge into producing a baby-milk formula suitable for newborns like Mary, and had begun training nurses at Seacliff in the best practices of childhood nutrition.

Truby's groundbreaking childcare techniques and ideas soon began to attract attention, and in 1907 he gave a lecture in Dunedin on the importance of nutritional health in women and young children. His idea was a simple one: establishing as secure as possible a start in life, by supporting new mothers and promoting childhood nutrition, would give the children of New Zealand the best possible chance of remaining physically and mentally healthy in adulthood. Like all the best ideas, it soon proved a near-instant success.

A Society for the Promotion of the Health of Women and Children was founded soon afterwards in Dunedin, which began advocating King's theories on childhood nutrition and post-natal care, for both mother and baby. Renamed the Plunket Society (when it gained the approval of the Governor of New Zealand's wife, and mother to eight children, Lady Victoria Plunket), before long the organisation's work had spread nationwide. It remains in operation to this day.

Just one question remains: what does all this have to do with Karitane?

It was in the sleepy seaside town of Karitane that Truby and Isabella King had a holiday home. There, they established a boarding house cum hospital, where babies could be treated and nurses could be trained under King's direction. As both King's work and that of the Society began to spread nationwide, the Karitane system went with it – and before long there were *Karitane* hospitals, *Karitane* nurses, and even a *Karitane* baby formula, just as Isabella had requested, available across New Zealand. By the 1920s, the town's name had become associated with all elements of ante- and post-natal care – and for all of this, in 1925, Truby King was knighted by King George V.

Of all Karitane's contributions to the language of childcare, however, perhaps this is the most striking:

> *Karitane yellow – an informal name for a (baby-excrement-coloured) unpleasant shade of yellow.*
> *—A Dictionary of Maori Words in New Zealand English*
> (2005)

And on that note, perhaps it's time to move on.

56

BIKINI ATOLL, MARSHALL ISLANDS

bikini

From New Zealand we take a four-thousand-mile trip practically due north, deep into the heart of the open Pacific Ocean. Our destination is a remote chain of twenty-three low-lying sandy islands surrounding a two-hundred-square-mile lagoon, in the far north of the Marshall Islands group. The atoll in question lies just north of the equator and just west of the International Date Line – so the local time here is a full twelve hours ahead of GMT.

The word under consideration isn't some obscure or little-known curio that matches the remoteness of the place. Far from it: the Marshall Islands' isolated Bikini Atoll is the etymological origin of the *bikini* swimsuit.

What connects the one to the other? Well, the answer to that lies with two French fashion designers and a US military project carried out at the atoll in 1946.

And Rita Hayworth.

On 1 July 1946, the US military dropped an atomic bomb nicknamed 'Gilda' (after Rita Hayworth's character in the film

Gilda, which had opened the previous February) on a fleet of ghost ships assembled as a target in the Bikini Atoll lagoon. The explosion – part of a series of nuclear tests in the area known as *Operation Crossroads* – marked the first major nuclear missile explosion since the bombing of Nagasaki the previous August, and was the first such test attended by an invited audience of military dignitaries, politicians and the press. The test was not quite the success the military had hoped for: the bomb landed a little off target, and damage to the ships was not as total as had been expected.* Nevertheless, the event was a spectacle unlike anything that had ever been seen before – and was soon being reported as such by the press, all around the world.

Eight thousand miles away in France, news of the US atomic bomb tests in the Pacific Ocean happened to coincide with the introduction of a new style of two-piece swimsuit, designed by Parisian fashion designer Jacques Heim. Skimpier than any

---

* A second test three weeks later, on 25 July, proved more destructive but still did not go entirely as expected. A bomb, nicknamed *Helen of Bikini*, was detonated underwater, throwing a vaporising column of contaminated sea spray high into the air, scattering radiation across the surrounding islands. Bikini was instantly rendered uninhabitable – despite the fact that the 167 Marshallese people who had lived there before being evacuated by the US military had been told they would be able to return after the tests were complete. Even after a lengthy clean-up operation, radiation levels at Bikini remain relatively high to this day; Glenn T. Seaborg (namesake of the element *seaborgium*, which we met earlier in the book) understandably called this second explosion at Bikini 'the world's first nuclear disaster'.

Today, the island has a permanent population of roughly half a dozen caretakers, who monitor radiation levels in the area. Conditions have improved in recent decades and Bikini has become a popular destination for scuba divers, who are drawn to explore the number of vessels sunk at the bottom of the lagoon.

similar swimsuit ever seen before, Heim named his design the *atome* – not only a buzzword of the nuclear age, but as the name of the smallest known unit of matter, a punning reference to the scantiness of Heim's swimsuit. Heim began selling his swimsuit in June 1946, several weeks before the first Marshall Islands test was carried out. Undoubtedly, it would have been his design – and, indeed, his name for it – that would have endured in the language, were it not for the work of fellow Parisian fashion designer Louis Réard.

Réard too had designed a similar two-piece swimsuit, and introduced his design at a fashion show four days *after* the first Bikini Atoll test had broken in the press. Perhaps partly inspired by Heim's *atome*, Réard named his design the *bikini* after the site of the recent nuclear test that was now known the world over. The design was even skimpier than Heim's – so much so, in fact, that Réard had to hire a nude dancer from a Paris casino to model it for the press. Made from a scant 30 inches of fabric, Réard marketed his design as 'smaller than the world's smallest swimsuit'; unlike Heim's *atome*, the *bikini* scandalously left the wearer's navel exposed.

Competition between the two designers and their swimsuits was soon afoot, but thanks to a mixture of good timing, better publicity and a growing appetite for more risqué designs in an increasingly liberated post-war Europe, it was Réard's bikini that eventually caught on. Despite initial controversy, his design has remained popular ever since – and has given the isolated Marshall Islands archipelago a surprisingly well-known place in our language.

57

KLONDIKE, CANADA

Klondike

From Bikini Atoll, we travel four and a half thousand miles across the Pacific Ocean to the far north of Canada, arriving just a few hundred miles outside the Arctic Circle for the story of a place whose numerous entries in our dictionary include a byword for a rich bounty or deposit; an untrustworthy madman; a single-player card game; a prison cell; and, probably most unusual of all, a word meaning 'to transport fresh rather than pickled herring'.

The location in question here is Klondike, the name of both a river, high up in the Canadian subarctic, and the area of land that surrounds it, not far from the Alaskan border. The Klondike flows for around a hundred miles through the hills of Canada's Yukon territory, before meeting the larger Yukon River at Dawson City. From there, it winds its way through Alaska and eventually empties out into the Bering Sea, more than seven hundred miles to the west. But how did this one isolated tributary come to have such a varied entry in the dictionary? It's simple: there's gold in them there hills . . .

The Klondike gold rush began in the August of 1896, when miners in the area discovered gold in the Klondike River (in a location now aptly named Bonanza Creek). As news of the discovery spread – eventually becoming known in the United States the following year – it triggered a mass migration of prospectors and gold-hunters keen to cash in on the find, and over the next three years, some hundred thousand adventurers made the journey from the USA to the Yukon Territory. In the two years from 1896 to 1898, the population of Dawson City alone increased from a little over five hundred to more than thirty thousand.

The gold rush, of course, didn't last. By 1899 the story had fallen out of the press, and as similar bounties began to be discovered elsewhere many of the prospectors moved on. The Klondike's time in the spotlight was over – but it had nevertheless left a lasting legacy on our language.

Just one year after gold was discovered in the area, the name *Klondike* had begun to be used as a byword for a treasure trove, or any similar mine or deposit of valuable material. *Klondike fever* had established itself as a general name for any gold rush, regardless of its location.

By the turn of the century, a form of the card game patience called *Klondike* had emerged, possibly because it was invented by or proved popular among the prospectors of the Klondike region. The sheer isolation of the area eventually led to the name being used among American criminals as a punning byword for a prison cell used for solitary confinement. And the madcap single-mindedness of Klondike prospectors, driven by nothing more than their desire for gold, had led to the name becoming a byword for madness or derangement:

> *Klondyke . . . Mad – not fit to be trusted. From the craze that set in August 1897 around the Klondyke gold-bearing district.*
> —J. R. Ware, *Passing English of the Victorian Era* (1909)

But of all the word's later meanings, however, perhaps the strangest or most unexpected emerged in Scotland in the 1920s:

Klondyke (v.) . . . to export fresh fish, mainly mackerel, to the
Continent, direct to factory ships for processing on board.
—*Dictionary of the Scots Language* (2004)

Precisely why the practice of selling and transporting fresh herring, and later mackerel, should become known as *Klondyking*
is unknown. Perhaps the term relates to the fact that these fish
needed to be packed and transported in ice, and an allusory reference to a distant place in the high Canadian subarctic somehow
fit the bill? Or perhaps this practice was so lucrative and could be
turned around so quickly compared to smoking or pickling, that
the get-rich-quick attitudes of the Klondike's gold prospectors
inspired its name? Whatever the reasoning, the term – perhaps
the strangest of all linguistic legacies of the Klondike gold rush
– remains in use to this day.

58

ADMIRALTY ISLAND, ALASKA, USA

hooch

From the Canadian Yukon we head almost five hundred miles south to the Alexander Archipelago, the mass of islands and islets that comprise the narrow fringe of land along Alaska's Pacific Ocean coast. At ninety miles in length and slightly larger than Majorca, Admiralty Island is among the largest of these thousand or so islands, and stands just a few miles from the mainland opposite the Alaskan capital city, Juneau.

Despite its proximity to the mainland, Admiralty is home to just over six hundred people, the majority of whom occupy a native Tlingit community called Angoon. So sparsely populated is this island wilderness that the brown bears here outnumber the local Tlingit population by three to one. Oddly, it's those two facts together that lie at the etymological root of the word in question.

The local Tlingit name for Admiralty Island is *Xootsnoowú*, which (perhaps unsurprisingly given the population statistics above) is said to mean 'fortress of the bears'. In the late 1800s, as the Tlingit became more closely integrated with the settlers and prospectors who ventured ever further into the Alaskan wilderness on the hunt for gold and furs, that local name fell into use in English in an array of anglicised forms, such as *Kootznahoo*, *Hootzenoo* and *Hoochinoo*.

Hoochinoo, ultimately, came to be used both as a colloquial name for the Tlingit settlement on Admiralty Island, and for the native Tlingit people who lived there. And, from the late 1870s onwards, it became attached to the eye-wateringly strong alcoholic spirit that the Tlingit brewed up on the island:

> *The name of firewater in Alaska is 'hoochinoo,' and recently the*
> *House [of Representatives] gave its official sanction to the word*
> *by enacting that no whisky, beer or 'hoochinoo' shall be sold in*
> *Alaska.*
> —*Boston Journal* (1899)

But *hoochinoo* is (literally) a bit of a mouthful. So, over the years that followed, it gradually simplified in form and spelling until by the turn of the century the Tlingit's firewater had become known simply as *hooch*.

Before long, that name had generalised in the language, acting as a byword in English slang for any doctored, poor-quality or impossibly strong alcoholic liquor. And we've had *hooch* – a word we owe to a remote bear-strewn island in the Alaskan wilderness – ever since.

59

HOLLYWOOD, CALIFORNIA, USA

Hollywood no

From Canada and Alaska we continue down North America's west coast to California, for the surprising story behind one of the most familiar words on our entire list: Hollywood.

Originally little more than a vacant collection of rural homesteads and orchards, during a real-estate boom in the late 1880s local ranch owners H. H. Wilcox and his wife Daeida began selling off acres of their land in the Hollywood area to investors and developers. The Wilcoxes made vast profits on each sale, and began channelling the money back into their own redevelopment projects in the area. Chiefly under Daeida's guidance, a fully functioning town soon emerged: a bank, post office, high school, police station, library, city hall and even a tennis club were all built in and around the burgeoning town of Hollywood, which despite a downturn in real-estate projects at the turn of the century – and the death of Daeida's husband in 1891 – continued to grow apace long into the early 1900s.

In 1911, the first of many film companies started operating in the area, and not long afterwards the iconic Hollywood sign was erected in the hills overlooking the town. Originally an advertisement for a new hilltop real-estate venture, the sign initially read 'HOLLYWOODLAND' and was intended to remain standing for only a year. Nevertheless it soon established itself as an iconic fixture of the town's landscape, and as the local film industry flourished in the 1910s and 1920s, both the name and the sign – and the town itself – became increasingly attached to the world of cinema in general.

The name *Hollywood** has consequently been used as a catch-all term for the entire American film industry† since the early

---

* Precisely why Hollywood is called *Hollywood* is a mystery. Perhaps the most outlandish, and certainly the most popular, explanation is that given by local real-estate developer and 'Father of Hollywood' H. J. Whitley. According to Whitley, while honeymooning in the hills around Los Angeles in 1886, he happened across a Chinese man who was collecting timber. When the two struck up a conversation and Whitley asked him what he was doing, the man replied, 'Hauling wood' – which, to Whitley's ears, sounded like 'Hollywood'. The combination of *holly* and *wood*, he reasoned, would make a fitting name for one of his developments, as he felt it neatly embodied both his English and Scottish heritage. Whitley was one of the earliest developers to take an interest in the Hollywood area, and, according to legend, his choice of name stuck. As compelling as Whitley's anecdote is, however, a more likely explanation is that the name was merely local landowner Daeida Wilcox's choice. She reportedly took inspiration from a lady she had a chance conversation with on a train one day, whose summer home was named 'Hollywood'.

† The use of a word (in this case *Hollywood*) to represent the entirety of something of which it is merely an associated part (in this case, the film industry en masse) is called *metonymy*. The same rhetorical process accounts for the likes of *Wall Street* being used to represent the entire US financial market; *Broadway* being applied to the entire theatrical industry; and New York's *Madison Avenue* representing the city's entire advertising industry.

1920s. But the name has also gone on to act as the inspiration for an array of phrases and expressions directly derived from it.

So the first *Hollywood ending* (an overly sentimental or unrealistic one) was described in 1929. The word *Hollywoodese* was coined in 1920, to refer to the jargony language of the filmmakers and creators of the Hollywood area, while the verb *Hollywoodise* first appeared in 1923 to mean 'to render glamorous'.

During the Second World War, the B-17 Flying Fortress appeared in so many movies that it became known as the *Hollywood bomber* in 1940s slang. A car's rolling stop at a stop sign or red light has been known as a *Hollywood stop* since the early 1980s – a reference to the way drivers in Hollywood movies rarely seem to stop or be held up in traffic on screen. And alluding to the ruthlessly uncompromising behaviour of Hollywood's agents and producers, a *Hollywood no* is a negative answer implied by an unreturned or unanswered telephone call.

60

JALAP, MEXICO

jalapeño

From California we cross America's southern border into a country whose etymological contributions to our language include a dog, a sauce, a chilli pepper, and – if legend is to be believed – a clapped-out old car.

The *Chihuahua* dog is the offspring of Mexico's Chihuahua state, where the breed has been selectively developed over centuries from the *techichi*, the favoured dog of the ancient Toltec people. *Sisal*, a fibre often used to make ropes and twine, is obtained from an agave plant of the same name, which in turn takes its name from a port in Mexico's Yucatan region from where it was once widely exported. And *Tabasco* sauce takes its name from the southern state of Tabasco – despite the fact that it was invented in Louisiana in the early 1800s. One of the sauce's main ingredients is the Tabasco pepper, a variety of chilli pepper native to southern Mexico that is said to have been introduced to the USA by an Irish-born New Orleans plantation owner named Maunsel White.*

---

* Maunsel White developed his own spicy sauce, called '1812', which he first served at a banquet celebrating his friend Andrew Jackson's victory in the War of 1812 and the Battle of New Orleans. The invention of modern Tabasco sauce, however, is credited to Maryland-born banker

The *jalapeño* pepper is another of Mexico's contributions to the dictionary, although its origins are a little less obvious. At the root of its name is the Mexican city of Xalapa, or Jalapa, the state capital of Veracruz, a hundred and fifty miles east of Mexico City. The city's name in turn derives from an Aztec word essentially meaning 'the sand by the water' – and the state of Veracruz, appropriately enough, forms one long strip of land along the coast of the Gulf of Mexico.

Long before the jalapeño pepper had English diners reaching for the ice water, the chilli peppers grown in Jalapa were used to make a strong purgative drug that was introduced to Europe in the seventeenth century as the *purga de Jalapa*, or *jalap*. Its earliest known description in English dates back to 1675, when the botanist Nehemiah Grew neatly outlined its effectiveness as a purgative:

> *Jalap hath a special property of irritating the glandulous parts of the mouth, and throat; we may gather, that it is a better purge to all the other glandulous parts than most other catharticks. Which is also one reason of its operation, for the most part, with at least a tendency to vomit; the stomach it self being glandulous as well as the throat, and thereby answerably affected with it.*
> —Nehemiah Grew, 'The Diversities and Causes of Tastes Chiefly in Plants' (1675)

And that was all the jalapeño had to offer the language for the next three centuries, until the first *jalapeños* began to arrive in the mid 1900s – although depending on your taste for spicy food,

Edmund McIlhenny, who developed his own recipe – likely inspired by White's, and using the Tabasco peppers he introduced from Mexico – in the mid 1860s. The McIlhenny Company still manufactures official Tabasco sauce to this day.

Nehemiah Grew's description above might be just as applicable today as it was back then.

So long as etymological legend is to be believed, however, it isn't just the *jalapeño* that we can thank the city of Jalapa for. Another theory claims that the word *jalopy*, meaning 'a worn-out car', takes its name from a corruption of Jalapa.

According to the story, battered old cars from the United States found a market for themselves in the south of Mexico, and ultimately many US vehicles ended up being sent to the area around Jalapa where they could be renovated and sold on, or else plundered for parts, or sold for scrap. *Jalapa*, among the English-speaking dealers who oversaw the trade across the border, gave rise to the slang name *jalopy* in the 1920s, which before long had established itself as a term for any clapped-out vehicle, useful only for scrap or parts.

That's just a theory, however – and there certainly are others.

If not derived from Jalapa, perhaps *jalopy* might derive from *chaloupe*, a French name for a small sailboat – although quite why that word should have been hauled up onto dry land and applied to a dilapidated car is unclear. A more plausible theory links *jalopy* to a Yiddish word, *shlepn*, meaning 'to drag' (from which the word *schlep* is derived), or else *shlappe*, meaning 'an old horse'. Perhaps *jalopy* is an English corruption of the Spanish word for 'tortoise', *galápago*, or else the Italian word for 'squanderer', *dilapidatore*, in the sense that a worn-out car needs ever more cash spent on it to maintain its roadworthiness. But of all the possible theories perhaps the best – though also perhaps the least likely – is that it represents a muddled blend of the word *jelly-apple*, a sweet treat once sold by Italian-American immigrants from rickety wooden carts.

61

SAN JOSÉ, COSTA RICA

Panlibhonco

From Jalapa we travel a thousand miles southeast, through the countries of Central America, and head to Costa Rica. The word that brings us here is one of the most peculiar on our list – and, admittedly, it's a word that we could have stopped in Liberia, Honduras, or else carried on to Panama, to talk about. That's because all four of these countries' names are bundled together in the obscure maritime term *Panlibhonco*.

Dating back to the 1950s, *Panlibhonco* is a seafaring and traders' term for a so-called 'flag of convenience' – a somewhat shady practice whose recent origins date back to 1919, and the age of Prohibition in the United States.

Under a 'flag of convenience', the owner of a ship records a vessel in the registry of a country not his or her own. The ship then flies the ensign of this host country – known as its 'flag' nation – regardless of its geographical origins.

On the surface, that might not seem too scandalous a custom. But if that 'flag' country happens to have looser regulatory laws than that of the ship owner's home country, then the implications (and, for that matter, motives) of a vessel using one of these 'flags of convenience' begin to become apparent. As the maritime registries of Panama, Liberia, Honduras and Costa Rica all happen to be among the most frequently used for precisely this kind of shady re-registering, it is these nations whose names have been ran together in the term *Panlibhonco*:

> *Since the end of World War II, shipping circles in the maritime countries have been watching with apprehension the increasing amount of merchant tonnage registered in Panama, Liberia, Honduras and Costa Rica (Panlibhonco), countries whose laws allow – and indeed make it easy for – ships owned by foreign nationals or companies to fly these flags.*
> —*Shipping World* (1957)

The practice of ships flying false flags is an ancient one, although historically the motive behind it was less driven by trade and more the need to secure victory in battle: ships flying the flag of their enemy could ultimately sail unnoticed amid enemy vessels, before launching a more close-quartered, and therefore more devastating, attack.

As a means of evading trade laws, however, the merchants' 'flag of convenience' is a much more recent invention. Its modern resurgence can be traced back to the USS *Zafiro*, a former collier and US Navy cargo ship that was reregistered in Panama in 1919 as the *Belen Quezada*, and used to transport alcohol into Prohibition America. Thus the *Belen Quezada* is credited with being the first modern vessel to fly under a flag of convenience, but it was by no means the last.

In the 1920s, many ship owners frustrated with the rising costs and increased regulation that followed the First World War began using flags of convenience to sidestep the most punishing maritime rules and protocols. As the practice grew, ever more countries around the world commenced their own open registries, attracted by the potential financial gains that an increase in trade could bring them. By the 1950s, the four nations bundled up in the name *Panlibhonco* had emerged as world leaders in this practice; by 1968 Liberia had surpassed even the UK as the world's largest marine registry.

Today, it's believed that around one fifth of the world's flags of convenience – more than eight thousand vessels – are still registered in Panama, while in terms of deadweight alone some 40 per cent of the gross tonnage of all ships at sea is registered in either Panama, Liberia or, now outdoing Honduras and Costa Rica, the Marshall Islands. Whatever the current world rankings, it is under the name *Panlibhonco* that vessels like these, and the questionable flags they fly, continue to be known.

Speaking of Panama, it's there that we're heading to next, continuing our journey south by another three hundred miles or so, into the southernmost country in mainland North America.

62

PANAMA CITY, PANAMA

Panama hat

Despite being the figurehead of the word *Panlibhonco*, perhaps Panama's greatest claim to etymological fame is the humble *Panama hat* – a style of high-topped and broad-brimmed straw hat, traditionally made from the dried leaves of the fantastically named jipijapa palm. Lightweight and breathable, the Panama is a popular choice of headgear in the tropical climate of Central and South America. It's just a shame that, despite its name, it's not actually from Panama.

The hats we now know as *Panamas* actually originated in Ecuador, seven hundred miles away, where a cottage industry built around weaving what were then known as *toquilla* hats (made from the leaves of local toquilla palms*) emerged in the seventeenth century.

---

* The toquilla's taxonomic name, *Carludovica palmata*, was given to the plant by Spanish botanists visiting Spain's South American colonies in the late eighteenth century. It was intended to combine the name of the then king of Spain, Carlos IV, and his consort Queen Ludovica.

These hats soon proved popular among locals and colonists alike, but failed to catch on much outside Latin America until the early nineteenth century. It was then, in the mid 1830s, that a Spanish entrepreneur named Manuel Alfaro arrived in the Ecuadorian city of Montecristi and, seeing commercial potential in the local straw hats, began to establish a chain of producers and sellers that could bring the hat to a broader market. Alfaro's trade route connected the local plantation workers and weavers in Ecuador, via the port of Guayaquil on Ecuador's southwest coast, with the ports on the Pacific coast of Panama. As more explorers, colonists and, later, gold prospectors arrived in the area – requiring a hat to shield themselves from the sun, while keeping their heads cool and ventilated – his business flourished, and the production of the hats expanded northwards into Central America, and southwards into the Andes.

By the 1840s, the hats had attracted the attention of traders in Panama, and were beginning to make their way back to Europe:

Are you aware of the beauties of a Panama hat? It is of fine straw – straw so fine and so exquisitely plaited, that it appears to be of one united glossy nature. It is as soft as silk, and as strong as chain-mail, and as elastic as caoutchouc. If you are caught in a shower of rain and your Panama gets wet through, you have only to wring it out as though it were a towel, and hang it on your walking-stick to dry, and in a quarter of an hour it will have regained its pristine shape. The Spaniards declare that a Panama is shot-proof, and an infallible protection against sunstroke; but of these assertions I have my doubts. The life of a Panama hat may be measured by that of a raven. It is supposed never to wear out.
—George Augustus Sala, *All The Year Round* (1866)

The Panama hat might not really have been bulletproof, but it was long-lasting and certainly popular. Unfortunately for poor old Ecuador, however, as the style's popularity grew, it took with it to Europe the name of the country from which it was sold and exported, rather than the country in which it had been invented and manufactured. As a result, it's as the *Panama*, rather than the *Ecuador*, that the hat has been known ever since.

That's also the reason why our next destination isn't Ecuador but rather its much larger neighbour to the south.

63

LIMA, PERU

Lima syndrome

Peru is the third-largest country in South America, sandwiched on the Pacific Ocean coast between Ecuador, Brazil, Bolivia and Chile.

The word Peru has donated to the dictionary has its roots in a city more than seven thousand miles away. On 23 August 1973, Jan-Erik Olsson walked into a branch of the Swedish high-street bank Kreditbanken in Stockholm and attempted to rob it. In the resulting stand-off with the Swedish police, Olsson took four people in the bank hostage, barricading them in the bank's vault. As the situation played out, Olsson requested that his friend (and fellow convicted bank robber) Clark Olofsson be brought from jail to the bank, along with 3 million Swedish kroner, guns and other weaponry, and a fast car in which they could escape.

Olofsson, whom the police believed could act as a mediator, was fetched, as was a suitable car. But when Olsson was told that he would not be able to take the hostages with him, he reacted angrily. He threatened to murder the four captives he had with him in the bank and relations with the police negotiators broke down.

As the situation escalated, Olsson was granted a telephone call to the Swedish prime minister, Olof Palme, during which he reiterated his threat. The following day, Palme again received a phone call from inside the bank but this time he spoke to one of the hostages, Kristin Ehnmark. By now, it was becoming clear that circumstances were starting to change.

As well as reiterating Olsson's demands, Ehnmark openly professed her concern not with Olsson's behaviour, but with the Swedish police's handling of the situation. 'I think you are sitting playing chequers with our lives,' she memorably explained to the prime minister, adding that she fully trusted her captors but was scared of what the police's actions might lead to.

Despite Ehnmark's concerns, when the situation once again failed to be resolved, the police resorted to drilling a hole through the wall of the vault, through which they began pumping tear-gas in an attempt to subdue all inside. Five days after the siege began, Olsson and Olofsson were apprehended, the hostages were released without serious injury, and the entire situation finally came to a dramatic end. Olsson went on to be sentenced to ten years in prison for the robbery, while Olofsson had his convictions quashed when the court agreed that he had indeed merely been trying to act as a go-between.

In the aftermath of the siege, the behaviour of those involved on all sides in the *Kreditbanken* robbery was analysed forensically. The curious sympathy the hostages appear to have developed towards Olsson and Olofsson fell under especial scrutiny, and led Nils Bejerot, a leading Swedish criminologist and psychiatrist, to coin the term *Stockholm syndrome*:* the psychological condition by which hostages come to sympathise with their captors.

This phenomenon was further expounded by the American psychologist Frank Ochberg, who identified *Stockholm syndrome* as almost a defence-like mechanism that kicks in in traumatic situations. The hostages, entirely beholden to their captors' every

---

* In Bejerot's original description, *Stockholm syndrome* was known as *Norrmalmstorgssyndromet*, or 'Norrmalmstorg syndrome' – after the town square in Stockholm, the Norrmalmstorg, where the robbery took place.

whim, see any act of generosity or kindness, no matter how insignificant, as somehow intensely meaningful, and in return form a strong bond of sympathy with them. In the Stockholm case, for instance, one of the hostages involved expressed profound gratitude that, when she admitted to feeling claustrophobic in the vault, Olsson had allowed her to walk around the lobby of the bank – even though he kept a rope tied around her neck the entire time.

In this way, *Stockholm syndrome* works as a survival technique: if the hostages are close to their captors, they are less likely to come to harm.

So what is it about a bank robbery in Sweden that has brought us seven thousand miles away to Peru? The answer to that, strangely enough, is yet another hostage situation.

At a little after 8 p.m. on 17 December 1996, a group of members from a Peruvian radical socialist group known as the Túpac Amaru Revolutionary Movement, stormed the residence of the Japanese ambassador in the Peruvian capital, Lima, during a high-profile party celebrating the birthday of the Japanese Emperor Akihito. Everyone attending the party – several hundred diplomatic workers, businessmen and government officials – was taken hostage.

Within twenty-four hours of the siege commencing, around half of the hostages had been released.

Three days later, another thirty-eight were freed.

And on 22 December another 255 hostages were released.

Many of those freed during these first few days of what would eventually be a prolonged ordeal were women and officials with little to do with the Peruvian government, but the reasoning behind their release is said to have been that the captors took pity on them, and regretted that they had become embroiled in actions they had little to do with.

The Lima siege would eventually go on to last 126 days, after which the ambassadorial residence was finally stormed by Peruvian special forces. One hostage, two Peruvian commandos, and all fourteen Túpac Amaru insurgents were killed. But this violent end to the events wasn't the only difference between this and the Stockholm incident. The apparent sympathy the hostage-takers had exhibited to many of the people they had taken captive led to the coining of the term *Lima syndrome* to describe the very opposite of Stockholm syndrome: the loss of resolve among the hostage-takers, who come to view those they have taken captive sympathetically.

The term has not quite gained the academic acceptance that *Stockholm syndrome* has and, unlike its Swedish equivalent, has yet to become much more widely known outside even the most obscure psychiatric journals. Nevertheless, the events that took place in Lima over the winter of 1996–7 helped to establish this little-known converse of *Stockholm syndrome* in the language and earned Peru a place in the dictionary.

64

STANLEY, FALKLAND ISLANDS

Falklands effect

F rom Peru we head almost three thousand miles away, across Chile, the Andes and Patagonia, to an isolated archipelago in the southern Atlantic Ocean.

The Falkland Islands lie around three hundred miles off the South American mainland, and their two main islands – East and West Falkland – plus their seven hundred smaller islands and islets are home to around three thousand people. Believed to have been uninhabited until as relatively recently as 1764, without human interference the islands' flora and fauna thrived, giving unique creatures such as the *Falkland Islands wolf*, the *Falkland steamer-duck*, and the herring-like *Falkland sprat* their own places in the dictionary.

And then, listed among all of those, there's the *Falklands effect*.

The bitter and long-standing dispute between the UK and Argentina over the sovereignty of the Falkland Islands came to a head in 1982 when, early on the morning of 2 April, Argentine forces invaded and occupied the islands, swiftly taking control of the official residence of the Falklands' British-appointed governor, Government House. The resulting Falklands War rumbled on for the next seventy-four days, eventually concluding with the surrender of the Argentine forces, and Britain reasserting its control of the territory.

The aftermath of the conflict was significant. In all, some nine hundred lives had been lost (including those of three Falkland Islanders). In Argentina, the ruling military government lost the confidence of the people, and as protestors took to the streets the regime collapsed, paving the way for the first democratic election in Argentina in a decade.

In the UK, meanwhile, support for Prime Minister Margaret Thatcher's Conservative government swelled. In the general election of June 1983 – held almost a year to the day after the conflict had ended – the Conservatives were re-elected in a landslide that saw them achieve their best election night result for forty-eight years.

The first four years of Margaret Thatcher's premiership had not been considered successful. Unemployment had increased, her party had fragmented, and the economy had struggled through a deep recession. For the Conservatives to achieve such a staggering electoral result in that context was highly surprising. But before long, it became clear what had reinvigorated the Tory vote.

Success in the Falklands War had led to a wave of patriotism sweeping across Great Britain, boosting confidence in the existing government. It was this that had secured Margaret Thatcher's victory and it was this that has become immortalised in the dictionary as the so-called *Falklands effect*, a term defined by the *Oxford English Dictionary* as 'the favourable effect on the popularity of a ruling party of conducting a foreign war'.

65

RIO DE JANEIRO, BRAZIL

Brazil nut

We return to the South American mainland from the Falkland Islands for the third and last of three chicken-and-egg etymologies. So far, we've found out that *turkeys* take their name from Turkey (but certainly didn't originate there), and that *canaries* take their name from the Canary Islands (which were themselves named after dogs). And last on our list is our next destination: two thousand miles north of the Falklands, in Rio de Janeiro on the southeast coast of Brazil.

The question is: which came first – *Brazil*, or the *Brazil nut*?

The earliest reference to the *Brazil nut* we know about comes from Alexander von Humboldt, who we first met way back in Switzerland. When he wasn't busy wandering the Jura mountains changing our understanding of geological history, Humboldt was off travelling around Latin America, touring the continent on a grand five-year expedition from 1799 to 1804. His first destination was New Granada, a vast Spanish-owned territory (roughly equivalent to modern-day Colombia, Venezuela and Ecuador) covering huge swathes of the South American rainforest. Accompanying him was the French botanist Aimé

211

Bonpland, and there, along the banks of the Orinoco River in Venezuela, the pair discovered an enormous species of tree that produced a large, strongly flavoured fruit.

Bonpland named it *Bertholletia excelsa* – *Bertholletia* in honour of his friend, the acclaimed French chemist Claude-Louis Berthollet, and *excelsa*, meaning 'glorified' or 'exalted' in Latin, a reference to the tree's extraordinary size. When the expedition was over and Humboldt returned home to Europe, he published an account of his travels, in which he had this to say about his discovery:

> *We lodged at San Carlos ... We found in the village a few juvia-trees which furnish the triangular nuts called in Europe the almonds of the Amazon, or Brazil-nuts. We have made it known by the name of Bertholletia excelsa.*
> —Alexander von Humboldt, *Personal Narrative of Travels to the Equinoctial Regions of America, During the Years 1799–1804, vol. 2* (1821)

By the early 1800s, then, not only had the Brazil nut itself arrived in Europe, but so too had its name. Except, however, that there's this:

> *Some of them are known for producing the Souari ... or Brazil Nuts of the shops, the kernel of which is one of the most delicious fruits of the nut kind that is known. An oil is extracted from them not inferior to that of the olive.*
> —John Lindley, *An Introduction to the Natural System of Botany* (1830)

This is the earliest English reference to a *Brazil nut* we know about (as Humboldt's *Personal Narrative* was not translated until 1852). But the fact that John Lindley, an English horticulturist and botanist, equates it with the *souari* nut causes us a problem.

The souari – also known as the *pekea*, or *butter-nut* – is the fruit of an entirely different species of tree, and is much flatter, broader, and softer-textured than the Brazil nut. This would seem to suggest that although Humboldt's account proves the *Brazil nut* had arrived in Europe by the early 1800s, at that time the name was probably originally a placeholder, referring to *any* large, edible nut that was imported from Spanish and Portuguese colonies in South America. Presumably, as the Brazil nut we know today became the more popular or most numerous species over time, it was to Humboldt's *Bertholletia excelsa* that the name *Brazil nut* came to be exclusively attached.

So in answer to the question of which came first, Brazil or the Brazil nut? The answer is certainly that the nuts were named after the country – it's just that the name probably originally wasn't quite as specific as it is today.

That still raises one final question, though: where does the name *Brazil* itself come from? Well, that is an even more complicated story . . .

Long before the Brazil nut arrived in the English language, back in the late 1300s the name *Brazil* was used to refer both to a tough brownish-red timber and a scarlet-coloured pigment, both of which were obtained from a tropical species of tree known as the *sappan*. The problem is, however, that the sappan is native to southeast Asia, not South America. So what happened there?

As the name of a mahogany-like timber, this fourteenth-century *brazil* derives from its French equivalent, *bresil*, which is in turn thought to have come from an ancient Germanic word meaning 'embers' or 'flames'* (a reference, perhaps, to the wood's rich, red colour). Originally, both the timber and the dye

---

* This, again, is just one of a number of etymological theories. If not derived from *brese*, an ancient word for 'embers', this *bresil* timber might take its name from another French word, *briser*, meaning 'to break' or 'crumble' (a reference perhaps to the wood drying out in transit),

obtained from it indeed came from southeast Asia. But as trade opened up with the New World as well as the Far East – and as similar timbers and dyes were discovered in the tropical forests of South America – *brazil* came to be use as a catch-all term for all hard red-brown timbers.

Over time, trade with the New World overtook trade with the Far East, and as the region became increasingly significant, on maps and charts from the mid 1500s onwards the coast of South America began to be listed as '*terra de brasil*' – literally, 'land of the red-wood dyes'. Brazil has been *Brazil* ever since.

But just when you think this etymology is solved, there's this:

Weste of yreland is an ylonde called the ilande of brasyll which stondeth in 51 degrees. Hit is almost rounde, of longitude it hath 12 leges and of latitude 9. ffrom Yreland to this yle of brasyll is 70 legis.

— Roger Barlow, *A Brief Summe of Geographie* (1541)

Clamber through all the jumbled early sixteenth-century English there, and you have a description of an island off the west coast of Ireland called *Brasyll*. Its author, Roger Barlow, was a companion of the explorer Sebastian Cabot, but he is here quoting data from a Spanish navigator and geographer named Martín Fernández de Enciso. He was born in Seville in 1470 – but the belief that an island named Brazil lay somewhere off the west coast of Ireland is even more ancient than that.

According to Irish folklore, *Hy-Breasil* was the name of a vast island in the north Atlantic Ocean that remained shrouded in mist except for one day every seven years; even then, on the one day it could be seen, the island was still unreachable. Its name apparently derived from that of an ancient Irish clan, whose

or *verzino*, an Italian-origin corruption of an Arabic name for saffron (in reference to the wood and the dye's rich hue).

name in turn was perhaps taken from an Old Irish word, *bres*, meaning 'mighty' or 'worthy'.

This legendary island first began to appear on maps and charts as far back as the 1300s, long before the *Brazil nut, brazil wood* or *terra de brasil* began to appear in English accounts. The myth has led to suggestions that early explorers of the Americas perhaps presumed that when they landed on the coast of South America they had finally reached this phantom island, and so Brazil – and ultimately the Brazil nut – took its name from ancient Irish folklore. It's an enticing story, certainly. But unfortunately, it's considered not to be the case.

When Portuguese explorers first set foot on Brazilian soil around 1500, they called it *Terra de Santa Cruz*, or 'Land of the Holy Cross' – making no reference at all to the curious mythical land west of Ireland. Unfortunately for the explorers, their choice of name did not last long, and within a matter of decades Terra de Santa Cruz had been all but replaced on European maps by *terra de brasil*.

So where does all that leave us? Well, the name *Brazil nut* certainly derives from Brazil – but, originally, it didn't refer only to the actual Brazil nut. As for Brazil, it took its name in turn from a tough, reddish timber and the dye extracted from it – only the tree and the dye in question came originally from southeast Asia. And you thought the journey we're currently on was complicated . . .

66

CAYENNE, FRENCH GUIANA

cayenne pepper

We now head to French Guiana, two thousand miles north of Rio de Janeiro, an overseas territory of France roughly the same size as Austria, on the far northeast coast of South America. As for the word we're here to consider, we're sticking with the culinary theme after the *Brazil nut*: the capital of French Guiana is named *Cayenne*.

We could be wading into another chicken-and-egg scenario: which came first, the *cayenne* pepper, or the city of *Cayenne*? But, mercifully, this story is a lot more straightforward than the *Brazil* vs *Brazil nut* debate we've just engaged in.

The cayenne pepper is a pungent, spicy-flavoured chilli pepper native to the forests of South America, often sold dried or ground into powder. Its name comes from a local Brazilian Tupí word, *kyynha*, essentially meaning 'pepper' or 'capsicum'. But the similarity between that native word and the name of the Guianan capital, *Cayenne*, apparently caused confusion, and as French Guiana became an ever more highly prized territory – changing hands repeatedly between the French, British and Dutch in the eighteenth and nineteenth centuries – its influence began to tell on the spelling of the pepper.

As a result, by the time the peppers were first being described in English in the mid 1700s, they were known by any one of a variety of similar names – including *cayan*, *kian*, *chian*, *chyan* and *kayan* – before the spelling finally standardised as *cayenne* around the turn of the century.

Two questions remain, then. First, if *cayenne* derives from *kyynha*, does that mean that *cayenne pepper* literally means 'pepper-pepper'? Yes. Yes, it does.

And second, where does the city name *Cayenne* itself come from? Founded in 1643 by French colonists, the city was given its present name in 1777; it's simply the old French form of the name 'Guyana'. As for the name *Guyana* – well, perhaps that's a story to leave for another day.* After all, the Caribbean is waiting . . .

---

* If you really want to know, *Guyana* is thought to come from a local Carib word meaning 'land of many waters'.

67

DAIQUIRÍ, CUBA

daiquiri cocktail

One of the popular explanations of the origin of the word *tobacco* is that it derives from the name of the island of Tobago, one half of the Commonwealth nation of Trinidad and Tobago:

> *This hearbe which commonly is called Tabaco, is an Hearbe of muche antiquitie ... The proper name of it amongest the Indians is Pecielt, for the name of Tabaco is geuen to it of our Spaniardes, by reason of an Ilande that is named Tabaco.*
> —John Frampton (trans.), *Three Bookes of Joyfull Newes* (1577)

This explanation by the Spanish botanist Nicolás Monardes is now considered etymological legend (as is the claim that Christopher Columbus named the island of *Tobago* because he fancied that its outline on maps looked like a smoker's pipe). Instead, *tobacco* is probably nothing more than a local Arawak Caribbean word meaning 'rolled leaves'.

Further north, one of the constituent islands of Antigua and Barbuda, Redonda, gave its name to a mineral discovered there, called *redondite*, in 1870. And, used as a verb, the name of the island of *Barbados* meant 'to transport convicts overseas' in seventeenth-century slang – a reference to the penal colonies of the Caribbean that were established there at the time.

Our next destination, however, lies much further north than all of these. From French Guiana we travel more than eighteen hundred miles northwest, heading to the largest of all the Caribbean islands: Cuba.

The name of the capital city of Cuba, Havana, on the island's far northwest coast, has been used as the name of a type of high-quality cigar since the early 1700s in English, while *havana-brown* established itself as the name of a rich earthy brown colour in the late nineteenth century. The *habanera* dance takes its name from the Spanish *danza habanera*, or 'Havanan dance'. But what brings us to Cuba now is a word whose origins lie in a small mining town on the opposite end of the island. The *daiquiri* cocktail – a mixture of rum, lime juice and sugar syrup – takes its name from Daiquirí, a village not far from Cuba's second-largest city, Santiago.

According to legend, the daiquiri was invented in a bar in Santiago either by or for a group of American mining engineers who had travelled to Cuba in the late 1800s to work at the Daiquirí mine. In one version of the story, the bar's owner ran out of gin while entertaining his wealthy American guests, and so was compelled to switch to an improvised rum-based cocktail to keep the drinks flowing. Another version of the tale credits an American engineer named Jennings Cox with its invention, claiming that it was he who ran out of gin while entertaining guests and, wary of serving the potent local rum neat, mixed it with citrus and sugar. And in yet another account, it was the engineers themselves, wanting to try the local Cuban rum, who drunkenly invented the cocktail and named it after the Daiquirí mine they had travelled to Cuba to oversee.

Whatever its true origins may be, the daiquiri cocktail's invention coincided with the outbreak of the Spanish–American War of 1898 – and Daiquirí, on the island's southernmost coast, proved the perfect disembarking point for the tens of thousands of American troops who were sent there to fight. The cocktail proved popular amid this new influx of American drinkers, and when the conflict was concluded a little over three months later, the recipe was taken back to the United States.

The daiquiri's popularity was further boosted when word of its recipe reached Washington DC's Army and Navy Club in 1909, a medical officer named Lucius W. Johnson being credited with its introduction there. The drink soon established itself as one of the most popular tipples of the Jazz Age, reaching its peak in the 1920s, and has remained enduringly popular ever since.

68

HAMILTON, BERMUDA

Bermuda

A thousand miles northeast of Cuba, and around nine hundred miles from the coast of North America, is the island of Bermuda in the north Atlantic Ocean. Like Cuba before it, Bermuda has given its name to a type of cigar, but also to the *Bermuda rig* (a method of arranging the masts and rigging of a sailing boat*); species of cedar tree, lily and marine grass; and the characteristically long-legged *Bermuda shorts*, which originated among the British Army for use in hot climates, and eventually proved especially popular on the island.

What brings us here now, however, is the story behind a considerably older term that first emerged in the street slang of London, some three and a half thousand miles away.

---

* Developed in Bermuda in the seventeenth century, the *Bermuda rig* remains perhaps the commonest configuration of a sailing boat's masts and rigging to this day. Because it requires a series of stabilising wires to support the mast and sails, this particular arrangement is also known as the *Marconi rig* in honour of Guglielmo Marconi, one of the inventors of radio transmission; the Bermuda rig's wires were said to resemble the telegraph wires Marconi's early telecommunications system used.

In the seventeenth and eighteenth centuries, the name of the island of Bermuda came to be used in what at first glance might seem to be a quite unexpected way:

> BERMUDAS . . . A cant term for certain obscure and intricate alleys, in which persons lodged who had occasion to live cheap or concealed . . . They are supposed to have been the narrow passages north of the Strand, near Covent-garden.
> —Robert Nares, A Glossary: Or, Collection of Words (1822)

The *Bermudas* of the eighteenth century were places where known criminals could hide from, or be free from the threat of, arrest. Like the ancient *Alsatia* of London's Whitefriars that we wandered into back in France, these *Bermudas* – or *Bermoothes* as they were also known – acted as asylums, and quickly became populated with all manner of rogues and villains. But why should such a shady word come to be associated with an island so far away?

A few decades after the island was first settled by the English in the early 1600s,* criminals and debtors in London looking to escape their crimes or arrears reportedly began fleeing the country for Bermuda – an island at such a great distance from England that surely no criminal or financial troubles could follow them. This practice apparently became well enough known

---

* The English settlement of Bermuda began with the shipwreck of the *Sea Venture*, part of a fleet of ships run by the Virginia Company, in July 1609. On its way to America, the *Sea Venture* was separated from the rest of its fleet by a storm, and deliberately shipwrecked on the eastern reefs off Bermuda, saving the lives of all 150 people on board. The extraordinary story is thought to have partly inspired Shakespeare's *The Tempest* (I.iii), which Shakespeare made reference to 'still-vex'd Bermoothes' as early as *c.* 1611. Today, the central image on the coat of arms of Bermuda depicts the shipwreck that inadvertently led to the island's colonisation.

to find its way into Ben Jonson's play *The Devil Is an Ass* (1616), in which one character complains that one of his debtors 'is run away to the Bermudas'.

Whether or not this practice ever *truly* occurred on any great enough scale to warrant a place in the language is debatable. (It's possible, alternatively, that as the name of some far-flung and exotic-sounding island, 'fleeing to Bermuda' was to many of these debtors and criminals little more than a figurative expression rather than a life choice.)

Nevertheless the term became attached to criminal hideouts and asylums in eighteenth-century London and remained in use in English right through to the early nineteenth century.

69

BUNCOMBE, NORTH CAROLINA, USA

bunkum

From Bermuda, we head a little over a thousand miles eastwards, returning to the mainland United States in order to hear a rambling political speech so unnecessary and tedious that it gave us a whole new word for 'incoherent nonsense'.

The fact that there's any kind of etymological connection between politics and long-winded speeches (or, for that matter, between politics and a word meaning 'incoherent nonsense') might come as little surprise. But the fact is that the word *bunkum*, or *bunk*, owes its existence to an insanely tedious speech delivered by US Congressman Felix Walker in 1820.

Born in Virginia in 1753, Walker was elected to Congress in 1817 as the representative for Buncombe County, North Carolina. He spent a total of six years in the House, during which time, in late 1819, Congress was tasked with debating the so-called Missouri Question: namely, whether the territory of Missouri should be admitted into the Union as a free or a slave state. The debate rumbled on for several inconclusive months, until finally, on 25 February 1820, just before the decisive vote was due to be taken and the matter put to bed once and for all, Congressman Walker stood to address the House. He went on to deliver a lengthy, rambling and largely irrelevant five-thousand-word speech. To put it into perspective, Walker's speech was almost as long as the entire role of King Lear.

It went on, and on, and on. And on. And, apparently, on. As the minutes ticked by, Walker's exasperated colleagues repeatedly shouted him down and yelled at him to desist but, undeterred, he continued talking. With a proud nod to his con-stituents back home in North Carolina, he explained that he was not 'speaking to the House, but to Buncombe'.

Oddly – and perhaps indicative of how unnecessary the rest of Walker's speech was – out of everything that he had to say that day, it was that pithy explanation that proved to be the most sig-nificant. Before long, saying or doing something 'for Buncombe' had slipped into political American slang to mean 'doing some-thing purely to please other people'.

By the mid 1800s, this expression was being used so widely that its original spelling, *Buncombe* – and its geographical connec-tion to North Carolina – was lost, replaced by a newly simplified phonetic spelling, *bunkum*. It was this that became a byword for political claptrap, empty promises and, eventually, utter nonsense.

Bunkum . . . (American) Talking for talking's sake, claptrap, gas, tall talk; orig. insincere political discussion. Hence . . . That's all bunkum = that's all nonsense! The thing's absurd!
—John S. Farmer and W. E. Henley, *Slang and Its Analogues Past and Present* (vol. 1, 1890)

A clipped form, *bunk*, followed in the early 1900s, and we've been *debunking* things by disproving or exposing them since 1923.

As for Congressman Walker, as well as earning himself and his congressional seat a place in the dictionary, he is still today commemorated on a plaque outside the town in North Carolina. 'Felix Walker, Revolutionary Officer,' it reads. 'Member of Congress, 1817–23, where in talking for Buncombe County, he gave new meaning to the word.'

70

NEW YORK, USA

tuxedo

On our way back north, we're bypassing all manner of intriguing words and phrases that could have made our final cut. In neighbouring South Carolina, for instance, we find the origin of the *Charleston* dance, the jaunty music which is thought to have originated among black dockworkers in the state capital of Charleston.

Bourbon, likewise, takes its name from Bourbon County in neighbouring Kentucky; the county in turn is said to take its name from the French royal house of Bourbon, after whose king, Louis XVI, it was named in recognition of his support for the American cause during the War of Independence.

Further up the coast, a *pocosin* is an area of marshland supposedly named after a low-lying river in eastern Virginia. A *Virginia fence*, meanwhile, is a barrier made by laying interlocking timbers one atop the other in a zigzag pattern; *to walk a Virginia fence*, in reference to its shape, is an eighteenth-century expression meaning 'to walk the zigzagging walk of a drunkard'.

Heading up into New England, a *monadnock* is an isolated peak or ridge that stands alone in an otherwise flat landscape, and takes its name from a Mount Monadnock in New Hampshire that is a prime example.

A *chautauqua* is an outdoor symposium of artistic and education events, so called as the very first symposium of this kind was organised at Chautauqua, in New York, in 1874. And we're staying in New York for the story behind how a tiny village on the New Jersey border gave its name to an item of fashion now known the world over.

Home to a little over six hundred people, the village in question is Tuxedo Park, in the southern corner of Orange County, New York. Tuxedo – whose name is thought to be an Algonquian word meaning 'crooked river' – was originally developed as a mining town in the late 1700s, but when the local iron deposits were exhausted the land was turned over to lumbering, before establishing itself as a hunting and fishing reserve in the late nineteenth century. It was around this time, in 1885, that the local landowner Pierre Lorillard IV (along with several well-to-do investors, including Viscount Astor) redeveloped Tuxedo Park into a luxury retreat for New York's wealthiest socialites. A clubhouse and numerous surrounding cottages and residences were built, and over time several new developments extended Tuxedo Park into a fully functioning village.

It was Lorillard's clubhouse that served as the focus of the resort, however – and it was there, in 1886, that a style of suit jacket that would eventually bear Tuxedo Park's name was finally introduced.

Credit for precisely who brought the *tuxedo* to Tuxedo Park is unclear. The style itself developed somewhat earlier than the mid 1880s, as a lighter, more casual, and tailless variety of the considerably more standard tailcoat. The Prince of Wales, later King Edward VII, is known to have worn a tailless coat of this kind that he had made for him by Henry Poole & Co., on Savile Row in London, and some stories claim it was the young prince who brought the style with him during a tour of America in 1860. Another story credits the style to Griswold Lorillard, Pierre Lorillard's son, who according to society newspapers at the time scandalously attended the 1886 autumn ball at Tuxedo Park wearing a 'tailless dress coat'.

But Tuxedo Park's own archives doubt both the prince's and Griswold's stake to the claim, and instead credit a merchant banker named James Brown Potter with introducing the style to the resort, having first come across it while working in London. No matter how the tuxedo jacket arrived at Tuxedo Park, however, and no matter who might be responsible for it, the style can hardly be said to have been an instant success.

Newspaper reports at the time decried the jacket as too informal to be of respectable use, and the scandalous style soon became associated with upstart *nouveau-riche* mavericks, and was rejected outright by American high society. Over the years that followed, however, that stance softened, so that by the 1890s the tuxedo's lighter, more casual style led to it being adopted as a summer, or less formal, alternative to the standard tailcoat.

With the brow-furrowing, pearl-clutching stigma that had been attached to it now gone, the tuxedo's popularity skyrocketed. And it has remained many people's black-tie style of choice ever since.

71

TORONTO, CANADA

Toronto blessing

Across Lake Ontario from New York state is the city of Toronto in Canada.

We might have been dealing with a lot of Old and Middle English, Latin and Ancient Greek, and eighteenth- and nineteenth-century slang, but the word that brings us to Toronto now is one of – if not the – most recent invention on our list. Dating from no earlier than 1994, a *Toronto blessing* is a fit of religious ecstasy.

On 20 January 1994, an Evangelical pastor from Missouri named Randy Clark was invited to minister to the congregation at the Toronto Airport Vineyard Church, or TAV.* Clark, whose congregation initially numbered just over a hundred church-goers, professed to have experienced miracles at churches he had spoken at before, and reported that he himself would often be overcome by the Holy Spirit during his ministry, falling into fits

---

* The church was later renamed the Toronto Airport Christian Fellowship Church, and finally rebranded as Catch The Fire Toronto in 2010. The church is now considered the flagship church of the non-denominational 'Catch the Fire' movement.

of spontaneous, ecstatic laughter. His words seemingly caught on with the small congregation in attendance that day, and before long many of those in attendance had fallen to the floor, shaking and laughing, crying, even barking and howling, in a seemingly otherworldly display. Clark assigned all these bizarre reactions to manifestations of the Holy Spirit entering the bodies of those in attendance. As news of the extraordinary display spread, his congregations grew.

Requested to minister at the church initially for only three days, Clark remained at the TAV for several months, during which time the size of his congregations increased tenfold as word of the events there spread. Before long, more than a thousand people were regularly packing themselves into the church, with ever more congregants experiencing the bizarre fits of religious ecstasy Clark's ministering inspired. Even more extraordinary, these fits appeared to be contagious; those in attendance who had travelled from miles around to attend Clark's meetings would reportedly bring this religious fever away with them, and similar instances of religious ecstasy began occurring elsewhere.

News of these events, and of Clark's work, understandably soon found its way into the press, and in an article in *The Times* in June 1994, the 'Toronto blessing' – which had apparently led 'one vicar . . . to cancel an evening service . . . remove the chairs from the nave because so many of his congregation were lying on the floor' in paralysed ecstasy – appeared in print for the very first time.

The impact of Clark's ministry was felt far outside the pages of the dictionary, of course. On the one hand, these extreme displays of religious fervour led to a revival of interest in the church in the mid 1990s, and reportedly led many agnostics and atheists to re-evaluate their relationship with Christianity. Clark's unorthodox methods did not go unnoticed by the established church, many of the members of which questioned, from a theological point of view, his focus on the power of the Holy Spirit over all else. Others merely questioned the veracity of his work, and that of the so-called *Toronto blessing* itself.

From its debut in print in 1994, however, the expression *Toronto blessing* has remained in use in the language in relation to the experiences at the Toronto Airport church ever since, but more recently it has also come to be used more broadly to refer to any instance of extreme religious ecstasy.

72

LABRADOR, CANADA

Labrador

Canada being the second-largest country in the world, we're somewhat spoilt for etymological choice. We could talk about the origins of *canola*, the vegetable oil – and the species of rapeseed from which it is made – whose name is at least partly derived from that of the country where it was developed. We could also talk about the origin of the expression *Canadian mosaic*, a term coined in the 1920s to refer to the patchwork of ethnicities and cultures that comprised twentieth-century Canada.

We could explain why Jerusalem artichokes* are also known as *Canada potatoes*, or why windcheaters are sometimes nicknamed *canadiennes* (spoiler alert: it's the weather). Or why a sofa that can be folded out into a double bed is known as a *Winnipeg couch* (spoiler alert: no one knows).

---

* There's a reason why the Jerusalem artichoke didn't make our itinerary: it has nothing at all to do with Jerusalem. In fact, its name is a corruption of the Italian word for a sunflower, *girasole*, which the artichoke is supposed to resemble.

But our final stop in North America before heading back across the Atlantic Ocean is the easternmost of Canada's thirteen provinces. Newfoundland, a former colony of Great Britain, rescinded its independence to become the tenth province to join the Canadian Confederation in 1933. In 2001 it officially changed its name to Newfoundland and Labrador to reflect the geographical and cultural divide that splits the region in two.

Geographically, the Labrador peninsula forms the province's mainland half, while the Atlantic island of Newfoundland comprises the rest. Despite being attached to the mainland, and despite being more than twice the size of its partner, Labrador has a population of just 27,000 people, compared to Newfoundland's 470,000. And culturally, while Newfoundland has long had historical ties to Europe and has welcomed many English, Scottish, Irish and French communities, Labrador is home to many native Inuit peoples.

The pair may have much to set them apart, but they do at least have one thing in common: both their names have since been given to two of the world's most popular dog breeds. And what's more, both breeds have a common ancestor on the island of Newfoundland.

The St John's water dog, also known as the 'lesser Newfoundland', was a working dog that originated on the island in the sixteenth century. Probably derived from a random cross-breeding of English, Irish and other European dogs that were brought to the island by colonists at the time, the St John's dogs were strongly built and fiercely intelligent, with dark brown or black fur, and distinctive white patches on the chest and chin. Many of these characteristics were passed on to the two breeds that eventually emerged from the St John's gene pool over the centuries that followed: on the one hand were the retrievers, including the modern Labrador and golden retriever, and on the other were the Newfoundlands.

As their name suggests, the heavier-built Newfoundland dog probably originated on the island of Newfoundland itself: native St John's water dogs were probably crossbred with mastiffs in the seventeenth and eighteenth centuries, increasing the breed's build and strength over time to create the Newfoundland. As for the Labradors, they were partly developed on the island and partly on the other side of the Atlantic Ocean in Great Britain.

After the first St John's dog that was brought to England arrived there in the early 1800s, breeding programmes were put in place to create a breed of retriever that was smart, fast and energetic. The breed that emerged kept the name of the dogs' ancestral home – and the first *Labradors* as we would recognise them today appeared in the mid 1800s.

73

GEYSIR, ICELAND

geyser

From Canada, we head more than fifteen hundred miles away to Iceland, breaking up our journey back across the Atlantic, for the story of how one of the world's most extraordinary geographical landmarks gave us a word for all other landmarks of that type.

Around fifty miles inland from the Icelandic capital, Reykjavík, in the far southwest of the island, is the Haukadalur valley, an area that includes some of Iceland's – and indeed the world's – most extraordinary geothermal activity. Among the valley's most celebrated sites are hot thermal springs and bubbling pools of natural mud, while the world-renowned Gullfoss waterfall lies just a few miles away to the north.

Two of the valley's most popular and most impressive attractions, however, are two vast thermal geysers, one of which, named Strokkur,* erupts regularly every five to ten minutes, while the other can lie dormant for several decades at a time. It is the second of this pair that concerns us here: described in geographical literature since the thirteenth century at least, it is

---

* Derived from the Icelandic for 'churn'.

known as the Great Geysir – and it is from it that all other geysers the world over have since taken their name.

Despite its international renown, however, this original
Geysir is surprisingly temperamental. Geological research suggests that it has been active for a staggering ten thousand years
– but that activity proves intermittent at best, and can often cease
altogether, for many years at a time, before being revived by
underground disturbance.

An earthquake in the Haukadalur area in 1896, for instance,
caused Geysir to erupt with remarkable ferocity for the first time
in many years. These eruptions lasted for many minutes at a
time, several times a day, casting a vast plume of boiling water
more than two hundred feet into the air. Geysir's renewed activity continued long into the twentieth century, with research in
1910 showing that even by then Geysir was still active as regularly as every half-hour. But by 1915, that regularity had slowed
to one eruption every five hours or so, and by the following year,
the activity at Geysir stopped altogether.

Over the years that followed, eruptions at Geysir were
occasionally artificially stimulated using chemical means,* but
it remained largely dormant again until another earthquake in
the area in 2000. Again, within a matter of years, this renewed
activity had subsided.

It may be temperamental, but Iceland's Great Geysir nevertheless proved impressive enough to earn itself a lasting place

---

* It is possible to prompt a geyser to erupt artificially by the addition
of simple soap or detergent. The soap disrupts the surface tension of the
water, allowing more water molecules held there to be released as steam,
and as the tension is released, so too is the pressure from the heated water
beneath. For a time, the Icelandic government permitted this to take
place every 17 June, on Iceland's National Day, before concerns over
the impact to the environment of adding soap to the thermal waters led
to the practice being stopped.

in our language. The name *Geysir* literally means 'gusher' in Icelandic, and derives from the equivalent Old Norse verb, *gøysa*, 'to gush'. Quite when the name was attached to the Great Geysir of Haukadalur is unclear, but the earliest reference to it in English at least dates from the mid 1700s. So impressive was this Icelandic Geysir that it quickly set the template for all other geothermal jets of water, and by the turn of the nineteenth century *geyser* had become the go-to English word for this type of landmark.

74

LIMERICK, IRELAND

limerick

From the geysers of Iceland, we head nine hundred miles south to Ireland, and a city whose contribution to our language is one of the most well-known entries on our entire list. Unless, that is, you'd rather believe the etymological folklore instead.

Look up the origin of the word *limerick* in the dictionary, and there's a good chance you'll be pointed in the direction of the English poet Edward Lear. Best known for writing *The Owl and The Pussycat* (1871), more than twenty years earlier Lear published an aptly titled *Book of Nonsense*:

> *There was an Old Man who said, 'Hush!'*
> *'I perceive a young bird in this bush!'*
> *When they said – 'Is it small?'*
> *He replied – 'Not at all!'*
> *'It is four times as big as the bush!'*
> —Edward Lear, *A Book of Nonsense* (1846)

Lear's book contained more than seventy five-line poems precisely like this one, each of which relayed the consistently bizarre

239

activities of a consistently bizarre parade of people – including 'an Old Man of New York' ('who murdered himself with a fork'), 'a Young Lady of Ryde' ('whose shoe-strings were seldom untied'), and 'an Old Person of Ischia' ('whose conduct grew friskier and friskier').

The collection proved hugely popular, and soon Lear's quirky five-line poems, each with its jaunty rhythm and memorable AABBA rhyme scheme, soon became known as 'Learic' verses. Over time, that fairly clumsy word *Learic* drifted ever closer to one of its more easily pronounceable soundalikes – *Limerick*, a city and county in southwestern Ireland. And eventually, it was this name that stuck.

It's a neat bit of etymological legend certainly, and it's an alluring story too. It's just a shame, rather fittingly, that it's complete nonsense.

For one thing, Lear didn't invent this AABBA style of verse. In fact, the earliest AABBA we know about can be credited to Thomas Aquinas, an Italian Dominican friar and scholar, who wrote these snappy lines in the mid thirteenth century:

> *Sit vitiorum meorum evacuatio*
> *Concupiscentae et libidinis exterminatio,*
> *Caritatis et patientiae,*
> *Humilitatis et obedientiae,*
> *Omniumque virtutum augmentatio.*

We're not dealing with some Latin tale about a man from Nantucket here. 'Sit vitiorum meorum evacuatio' is actually a prayer:

> *Let it be for the elimination of my sins,*
> *For the expulsion of the desire and lust,*
> *For the increase of charity and patience,*
> *Humility and obedience,*
> *As well as all virtue.*

Aquinas didn't call his prayer a *limerick* of course – but then again, neither did Lear.

Another problem with the idea that *limerick* derives from Edward Lear's 'Learic' verse is that in relation to a five-line poem *limerick* didn't appear in print until 1896, some eight years after Lear's death. It was then that the author and artist Aubrey Beardsley wrote a letter to a friend to say that he had been trying 'to amuse myself by writing limericks on my troubles'.

The limerick Beardsley came up with, inspired by a painting of St Rose of Lima, is far, far too indecent to be printed here. (After all, there might be children reading this.) So if you want to know more head to the footnote,* or else search for it online if you really want that sort of thing in your browser history.

Late nineteenth-century smut to one side, what concerns us here is that thirty-two-year gap between Lear's collection of poetry in 1864, and Beardsley's use of the term in 1896. Tellingly, Beardsley uses the word freely, and without the need for any elucidation, which suggests that the word *limerick* was already familiar as the name of an AABBA poem by the time of his writing. Is thirty years long enough for *Learic* to morph into *Limerick*? If Lear was single-handedly responsible for its invention, then surely there would be more evidence in between? Both of those questions cast even more doubt on Lear's involvement.

So where did the name come from if not from Edward Lear? Well, as is often the case with etymological mysteries like this, the simplest explanation is the most likely: the *limerick* poem takes its name from *Limerick*, Ireland.

---

* St Rose, according to Beardsley's poem, 'played dirty tricks / With a large crucifix' – and let's not dwell on this any further, except to say that on the final line Beardsley manages to rhyme 'Lima' with 'femur'. On an entirely unrelated note, St Rose is the patron saint of those ridiculed for their piety.

There was once an old drinking game, popular in the late nineteenth century among troops in the British Army, that required all those taking part to make up their own verse of an ever lengthening song, one person after another. Each verse consisted of an improvised five-line poem with AABBA rhyme scheme, with the chief rule being that the verse should be witty, nonsensical, satirical, or as indecent in nature as possible. And in between all of these spur-of-the-moment verses, the entire group together would combine their voices for the chorus, 'Will you come up to Limerick?'

The game is believed to have been based on an earlier Irish jig called 'Will You Come Down to Limerick?', or 'Kitty Come Down to Limerick', the tune of which would have provided the verses with their melody. The jig is still performed (albeit without the indecent lyrics, one hopes) today.

So the familiar five-line *limerick* – etymologically at least – has nothing to do with the great Edward Lear, despite it being a style of poetry forever associated with his nonsensical verses. Instead, we can thank, somewhat indirectly, the soldiers of the British Army, and the otherwise blissfully unaware city of Limerick.

75

DUBLIN, IRELAND

donnybrook

W
e're off to Dublin – or, more specifically, to what is now a suburb of Dublin, in the south of the city, whose ancient name has entered the dictionary as a slang term for a scene of uproar or disorder.

In 1204, King John chartered a licence to the city of Dublin to hold an annual agricultural fair in Donnybrook, then a rural area to the south of the city. Initially an eight-day affair where livestock and farm produce could be bought and sold, the fair proved such a success that by the mid thirteenth century its duration had been extended to two weeks. From there, it endured for the next six hundred years, until the fair was unceremoniously cancelled, held for the final time in 1855. So what happened in between to bring about the Donnybrook Fair's downfall?

As the years went by, the crux of the fair moved away from agricultural trading and more towards drunkenness and debauchery. To keep the festival-goers fed and watered, stalls selling beer and whiskey were permitted, and as each two-week fair went on those attending began to, shall we say, spend more time enjoying what these stalls had to offer than anything else there. By the nineteenth century, the fair had grown to a colossal size, with people travelling from far and wide from across Ireland and beyond to celebrate the end of the summer with a two-week period of drunkenness and debauchery. It's by no means a coincidence that in the days leading up to the start of the fair, banks and pawnbrokers in the city of Dublin reported better business than at any time of the year, while in the weeks after the fair, the local hospitals were grossly overcrowded:*

> *This annual scene of profligacy and drunkenness is held during the last week in August, and is commenced on a Sunday. The fair green is situated at the south-east extremity of the suburbs of Dublin. There are generally from two to three hundred tents erected, in all of which, besides public houses in the neighbourhood, the worst description of whisky is sold. Each tent is provided with a piper or fiddler, and a board for dancing. The fair ... is frequented not only by the thieves and prostitutes of Dublin, but even by shopkeepers, tradesmen, and their wives and children, and by domestic servants.*
>
> —John Dunlop, *Artificial and Compulsory Drinking Usages of the United Kingdom* (1844)

It might not be surprising to discover that the founder of the British temperance movement, John Dunlop, did not find much to his pleasure at Donnybrook. He was by no means alone. One anonymous nineteenth-century writer claimed to have found, 'amidst mere merriment and mirth ... more misery and madness, devilment and debauchery, than could be found crowded into an equal space of ground in any other part of our globe'.

---

* To give an idea of the level of drunkenness revellers at Donnybrook achieved, one mid-nineteenth-century hospital report records one man who had been 'lying on the damp ground all night in a state of inebriation', who had awoken to find 'his face almost eaten off by a pig'.

German nobleman Hermann, Prince Pückler-Muskau, who toured the United Kingdom in the nineteenth century, wrote that he, 'saw things eaten and drunk with delight' at Donnybrook that 'forced me to turn my head quickly away to remain master of my disgust'. Quite what he witnessed being eaten, mercifully (or frustratingly, depending on how you look at it) he did not say. And even the entry for Donnybrook in the official *Parliamentary Gazetteer of Ireland* (1846) described it as a fair 'professedly for the sale of horses and black cattle, but really for vulgar dissipation . . . criminal outrage, and the most revolting debauchery'.

But there's only so much drunkenness, prostitution and porcine face-eating that one city can take, and eventually a burgeoning movement emerged in Dublin to bring the Donnybrook Fair to a close.

By the eighteenth century, the licence for holding the Donnybrook Fair had passed to one Henry Ussher, who passed away in 1756. On his death, the licence was bequeathed to a William Wolsey, who in 1812 sold it to a gentleman named John Madden. By the turn of the nineteenth century, however, an official Committee for the Abolition of Donnybrook Fair had been established in Dublin, its aim being to raise enough money to purchase the licence from its current holder and axe the fair once and for all. Eventually, they achieved their goal: in 1855, the licence was purchased from John Madden for the princely sum of £3,000 (equivalent to more than £300,000 today), and the fair was never held again.

By then, however, the damage was done. *Donnybrook* had already passed into general use in the language as a metaphor for any similar scene of drunkenness or profligacy, and in this figurative sense was first recorded in 1852 – a full three years before the committee to abolish the fair succeeded in its quest. The word has remained in use ever since.

76

GLASGOW, UK

Glasgow magistrate

From Ireland we cross the Irish Sea, heading for Scotland. Unsurprisingly, now that we're on home soil, we've a lot more etymological and linguistic gold to mine.

Of all of the Scottish map's etymological exports, perhaps the most famous is *paisley*, the name of an ornamental design using a characteristic teardrop pattern,* taken from the Scottish town outside Glasgow where the intricately patterned fabric was once manufactured. Equally well known are *Dundee cakes*, rich fruitcakes, traditionally topped with a concentric design of almonds,† said to have originated in the city of Dundee. And *Edinburgh rock* was invented in Edinburgh in the mid nineteenth century, by adding cream of tartar to the traditional sugar-rock recipe.

---

* The teardrop on paisley fabric is called a *botah*, and is Persian in origin. Originally imported into Britain and Europe from Central Asia, fabrics and shawls bearing this design proved hugely popular in the eighteenth and nineteenth centuries, leading fabric manufacturers in Paisley to replicate the pattern in an attempt to monopolise on the trend.

† According to legend, Dundee cakes' traditional almond-covered tops were first produced for Mary, Queen of Scots, as a replacement for more typical glacé cherries, which she did not like.

At the more obscure end of the lexicographic scale are a number of ever more arcane local dialect expressions and proverbs, like a *Skyreburn warning*,* a proverbial expression for no warning at all, especially in instances of gross misfortune. It alludes to a stream in Galloway, the Skyre Burn, which once had a reputation for flooding swiftly and unexpectedly.

All to one side, like Gourock, is an expression of lopsidedness that namechecks the port of Gourock on the Firth of Clyde, which stands almost entirely on one side of a steep hill. And the proverb *he that can hear Dumbuck may hear Dumbarton* refers to the proximity of two locations on the outskirts of Glasgow:

> *Dumbuck Hill in Argyllshire is farther from Glasgow (the locale of this saying) than Dumbarton: proverbially [it is] applied to those who are better acquainted with circumstances than they pretend to be, but who, in their anxiety to gain more information, betray themselves.*
> —Alexander Hislop, *The Proverbs of Scotland* (1862)

Speaking of Glasgow, of all the entries in the dictionary that namecheck a Scottish town or city, perhaps the most peculiar of all is the *Glasgow magistrate* – an early nineteenth-century nickname for a herring. Where did such a peculiar expression come from? Admittedly, no one is entirely sure. But there are at least a few explanations; it's just that one is ever so slightly fishier than the other.

---

* It's possible that this expression was also coined in response to an earlier expression, a *Scarborough warning*, of similar meaning. According to etymological lore, this earlier phrase alludes to an occasion in 1557 when the rebellious Thomas Stafford stormed the Yorkshire town of Scarborough and occupied its castle before any of the townspeople had even realised. Stafford, who led two rebellions against Mary I, was eventually executed for treason later the same year.

On the more plausible side here, there is this:

Herring were cured there by Walter Gibson, a merchant of Glasgow and Provost of that city in 1688, and it is perhaps because of Provost Gibson that salt herring acquired their nick-name of 'Glasgow Magistrates'.
—*Scots Magazine* (1950)

A gentleman named Walter Gibson did indeed help to establish Glasgow's lucrative herring industry in the late seventeenth century, and he did indeed become provost (chief magistrate) of the city in 1688. But is he really the origin of the term? And is the establishment of a herring-curing factory really the most entertaining story we have on offer here? No. No, it's really not.

The problem is that if Walter Gibson were the original *Glasgow magistrate*, we'd have to accept a century-and-a-half gap between his appointment as provost in 1688, and the earliest written record of the phrase in print, which the *Oxford English Dictionary* traces to 1833. That'd be by no means impossible, of course, as slang and dialect expressions are used relatively seldom in print. But it nevertheless casts doubt over the Walter Gibson theory, and it all becomes a lot more doubtful given the other explanation on offer.

In a revised edition of his *Dictionary of Phrase and Fable* (1894), the lexicographer E. C. Brewer included the expression *Glasgow magistrate* (alongside *Yarmouth capon* and *Billingsgate pheasant*) as a nickname for a salted herring. He also offered this brief, yet brilliant, account of its possible etymological origins:

When George IV visited Glasgow, some wag placed a salt herring on the iron guard of the carriage of a well-known magistrate, who formed one of the deputation to receive him.

Quite where or how Brewer came across this story isn't clear, but he does go on to explain:

> *I remember a similar joke played on a magistrate because he said, during a time of great scarcity, he wondered why the poor did not eat salt herrings, which he himself found very appetising.*

So is this tale of a local Glaswegian scallywag secreting a herring onto a processional carriage true? Well, by namechecking George IV, Brewer is certainly proposing a date that seems to fit with the evidence: George took to the throne in 1820 and reigned for the next ten years, so written evidence dating from around 1833 is perfectly reasonable. There is, however, a problem: King George visited Scotland only once in his ten-year reign – and he never set foot in Glasgow.

In 1822, George IV became the first Hanoverian monarch – as well as the first reigning monarch in nearly two hundred years – to visit Scotland, when he stayed in Edinburgh for three weeks in mid August. During that time, the king attended all sorts of predictably glamorous pageants and processions – all stage-managed by Sir Walter Scott, no less – and throughout it all reportedly managed to make a complete fool of himself by opting to wear bright pink stockings under a criminally undersized kilt in an attempt to fit in.

At no point, however, did he make the journey to Glasgow.

Does this fact blow Brewer's fishy theory out of the water? Perhaps not. We know that some 300,000 Scottish people – a staggering one in seven of the entire population at the time – turned out to see the various events put on for the royal visit in Edinburgh in 1822. And we also know that a large proportion of all those who attended had made the short forty-mile trip from Glasgow, as it was reported at the time that the city had been left all but deserted.

So could it be that Brewer's Glaswegian prankster was in fact among the crowds in Edinburgh, rather than in his home city? And that somehow the city's names became crossed at some point in their history? It's not only plausible, but it's a much better story.

77

NEWCASTLE UPON TYNE, UK

Newcastle programme

We leave Scotland and head south, pausing in the city of Newcastle upon Tyne in the northeast corner of England.

As far as the dictionary is concerned, arguably Newcastle is most familiar thanks to the expression *to take coals to Newcastle*. Dating back to the early 1600s at least (although an alternative expression, *as common as coals in Newcastle*, is apparently even older), the phrase is one of a number of similar expressions alluding to a pointless folly or entirely superfluous activity. Newcastle is naturally so coal-rich, the expression advises, that taking any more there would be utterly and foolishly unnecessary.*

---

* This is just the latest in a long line of expressions along these lines, many of which date back into antiquity. Even the Ancient Greeks got in on the act: owls once roosted in such numbers in the Athenian Parthenon – and, as a symbol of Athena, were stamped on all the city's coinage – that taking owls to Athens was a proverbial expression of superfluousness. Whether it was intended to refer to the coins or the actual birds themselves (or, for that matter, both) is impossible to say.

At the less familiar end of the scale, *Newcastle hospitality* is a nineteenth-century expression for what one 1893 dictionary of *Northumberland Words* defined as 'roasting a friend to death' – or what we might now call (in somewhat less dramatic words) 'killing with kindness'.

And then, of course, there's this:

Newcastle programme. (1894 on). Extreme promises, difficult of execution.
—J. R. Ware, *Passing English of the Victorian Era* (1909)

So how did the city of Newcastle come to be associated with promises that are impossible to keep?

In 1891, an annual conference of all Liberal Party associations in England and Wales was held in Newcastle upon Tyne, fronted by Liberal leader (and three-time former prime minister) William Gladstone. The centrepiece of the conference was an outlining, step by step, of all the Liberal Party's political policies that they should look to implement should they win the following year's general election. Among the raft of radical reforms included on the Liberal agenda were such forward-thinking policies as employers' liability for workplace accidents; a reduction of factory working hours; free education; a reform of the House of Lords; the abolition of so-called 'plural voting' (which had hitherto allowed certain individuals to cast more than one electoral vote) and numerous changes to local district and parish councils. But of all the Liberal Party's aims, of greatest significance was a resolution to establish Home Rule in Ireland.

The Newcastle Programme, as it became known, was ultimately akin to a modern party manifesto: the aims of the party were plainly itemised, giving the electorate a clear breakdown of all that they would seek to achieve, should the party win their vote. As an electioneering tactic, it was groundbreaking. In practice, it proved disastrous.

The 1892 general election ended with no party winning a clear majority, but Gladstone's Liberals hugely increased their standing in the House of Commons by securing a total of eighty-one new seats. So with no outright winner, and with the incumbent Conservative prime minister, the Marquess of Salisbury, facing a vote of no confidence, Gladstone stepped up and engineered a minority parliament. His Liberal Party would rule with him installed as prime minister for a record fourth time – but the entire arrangement relied on the Irish National Federation propping his government up, and affording him the seventy-two seats they themselves had secured.*

Gladstone's collaboration with the INF thrust his party's promise to further home rule in Ireland into the political spotlight. But he had a problem: the House of Lords, the UK's higher parliamentary chamber, still had a clear Conservative majority.

Gladstone's party passed a Home Rule Bill for Ireland the following year, but when the bill was handed to the Lords for ratification, it was rejected. His government was quickly placed in stalemate.

With home rule for Ireland now its chief concern, many in Gladstone's party – and many of those who supported it – now found their domestic concerns increasingly disregarded, at the expense of achieving the chief promise of the Newcastle Programme and thereby maintaining the support of the INF. The Conservative hold on the Lords, meanwhile, made the passing of

---

* The Liberals secured a total of 272 parliamentary seats in 1892 election, compared to the 313 won by Salisbury's Conservatives. At the time there were 670 seats available in the House of Commons, meaning a total of 336 was required to secure a parliamentary majority. By joining forces with the Irish National Federation and securing the support of its 72 seats, Gladstone both claimed his majority and his record fourth term as prime minister. Then aged eighty-two, he also became the oldest person in history to hold the office.

any new Liberal policies all but impossible. Splits and factions began to emerge in the party, and as the entire situation calcified, Gladstone was compelled to resign in March 1894, less than two years after taking office. The following year, after an overwhelming defeat in the 1895 election, the Liberals' Newcastle Programme of promises was abandoned.

Having proved all but impossible to keep, the name of the programme fell into use for a short time in turn-of-the-century slang, to refer to any promise or agreement that in practice proves unimplementable.

Newcastle has one more linguistic claim to fame on offer – for that story, we first need to travel a hundred and fifty miles south . . .

78

GOTHAM, UK

Gothamite

The tiny village of Gotham in Nottinghamshire, central England, is the next stop on our list. From the outside looking in, it is a picturesque, entirely unassuming rural English village, nestled between the River Trent to the south, and the city of Nottingham to the north. To look at it, you wouldn't think that it had given its name to one of the most famous – and entirely fictitious – cities in the world. Yes, this really is the story of Gotham City. But no, this particular tale doesn't begin with a bungled robbery in an inner-city alleyway. Instead, we're back in Tudor England . . .

Sometime around the mid fifteenth century, the name *Gotham* began to be used as a byword for any unsophisticated backwater town or village whose populace was all proverbially foolish, bumpkin-like characters. The earliest record we have of that comes from one of the Wakefield Mystery Plays, a series of thirty-two religious plays first performed in Wakefield, in West Yorkshire, sometime in the mid 1400s. We know from the only surviving script of these plays that at least one of them contained the line, 'foles all sam, Sagh I never none so fare, Bot the foles of Gotham'; take that impenetrably jumbled Middle English and bring it bang up-to-date, and you'll have something along the lines of, 'They're all fools. I never saw a fool so fair [game] as the fools of Gotham.'

This allusion became so widespread in Tudor English that in 1540 an entire book of comic anecdotes about the ironically named 'Wise Men of Gotham' was published. In one of the stories, one particularly foolhardy Gothamite rides his horse while carrying a huge sack of grain on his back so that the horse doesn't have to carry all the weight. In another, a gang of Gothamites decides to punish an eel that has eaten all the fish in a local pond by trying to drown it. Eventually, the joke became so widespread that it even inspired a sixteenth-century folk rhyme, which described the hapless misadventures of three wannabe seamen from Gotham:

> *Three wise men of Gotham,*
> *Went to sea in a bowl.*
> *Had the bowl been stronger,*
> *My song'd been longer.*

Admittedly, it's unclear whether or not this proverbially foolish 'Gotham' was actually based on the real-life village of Gotham* or was merely a fictional invention, but the Nottinghamshire Gotham is widely considered the most likely candidate. Being known for your proverbial stupidity isn't the most welcome legacy a town could leave on the linguistic landscape, but happily it's not all bad news. Things began to change around the turn of the eighteenth century.

It was around then that *Gotham* began to be used as a nickname for any town whose inhabitants were (albeit very unfairly)

---

* Etymological connections have also been drawn to a long-lost 'Gotham Hall' in the county of Essex, the proximity of which to the capital might have made its relatively rustic inhabitants a prime target for jokes among the more urbane Londoners nearby. But if that's the case, it's doubtful that the earliest written record of *Gotham* would appear two hundred miles away in Wakefield.

viewed as being less sophisticated or less cultured than those of larger, more cosmopolitan cities. In this context, the nickname *Gotham* was probably applied to any number of different places across England including, among them, Newcastle upon Tyne. But, by then, all those old-fashioned Tudor folktales and folk rhymes had started to fall out of fashion, and as they vanished from memory the name *Gotham* began to lose all its negative connotations. By the nineteenth century, it was being used merely as a byword for any large town or city, regardless of the sophistication of the people who lived there. And in that context, it remained particularly associated with Newcastle:

> *Heav'n prosper thee, Gotham! thou famous old town,*
> *Of the Tyne the chief glory and pride:*
> *May thy heroes acquire immortal renown,*
> *In the dead field of Mars, when they're try'd:*
> *Amongst them, O ne'er may a flincher be found;*
> *And that mirth they from duty may draw,*
> *Long, long, through their ranks may these accents resound,*
> *'Kiver awa', Kiver awa', Kiver awa'.'*
> —*Rhymes of Northern Bards* (1812)

Those are the lyrics to a Newcastle ballad called 'Kiver Awa',* which, according to the collection in which it appeared, was written in November 1804. The 'Gotham of the Tyne' mentioned here is, unsurprisingly, the city of Newcastle upon Tyne, and this obscure ballad proves two things.

Firstly, given the glowing praise these lyrics heap on the city, by the turn of the nineteenth century we can tell that Gotham is a name that has been all but embraced by the city, and lost all of its earlier negative connotations. And secondly, as this ballad

---

* 'A command used in drilling', according to the *English Dialect Dictionary* (vol. 3, 1905)

provides us with the earliest known written reference to any city anywhere being labelled 'Gotham', the very first 'Gotham City' was Newcastle upon Tyne.

To most people today, however, *Gotham* has firmly established itself as a nickname for New York. So at what point did the name make its leap across the Atlantic?

English emigrants are presumed to have taken *Gotham* – by that time simply an old nickname for a large city – across to America in the early 1800s, and there began using it in reference to New York City. In that sense, it first appeared in print in the United States in an instalment of the author and journalist Washington Irving's satirical magazine *Salmagundi* in November 1807, which made reference for the first time to 'the chronicles of the renowned and antient [*sic*] city of Gotham'.

For Irving's article to have made sense to its readers, we can presume that the nickname *Gotham* was already fairly well established in New York by the time he came to use it. There, over the years that followed, its use in reference to the city of New York blossomed, while over in England the nickname largely disappeared. By the turn of the century, the word had completed its extraordinary journey from rural Nottinghamshire, to the shores of the River Tyne, and finally across the Atlantic Ocean to New York.

79

COVENTRY, UK

send to Coventry

Our penultimate stop is just a short thirty-four-mile journey from Gotham (the Nottinghamshire one, that is, not the New York one). We're heading for the city of Coventry – but, thankfully, we're going of our own volition. We've certainly not been *sent* there.

People who are ostracised or excluded from a group have been figuratively *sent to Coventry* for over three hundred years. Back then, when this phrase is supposed to have emerged in the seventeenth century, Coventry was still a relatively small town. But, according to etymological legend, it was nevertheless significant enough to warrant playing quite a considerable role in an event of the English Civil War.

In *The History of the Rebellion* (1702–4), a first-hand account of the Civil War written by Edward Hyde, the Earl of Clarendon, a group of Royalist troops apprehended in the city of Birmingham is recorded as having been taken to nearby Coventry to be imprisoned. At the time of the conflict, Coventry was a parliamentarian stronghold, and as a result the arrival of some of the king's Royalist troops in the town would hardly have been met with a warm welcome from the residents. As a result, the Royalists were widely derided and shunned throughout the town and, according to etymological lore, it was this mistreatment that led to an ostracised person being said to be *sent to Coventry*.

But then again, maybe it wasn't.

The Earl of Clarendon's anecdote is certainly a compelling etymological tale, and it's by no means an implausible one either. The only problem is that there is no etymological evidence, other than the details of the story itself, to support its popular claim as the rightful origin of being *sent to Coventry*.

But there's actually very little written evidence of *anything* that might give us a clue to the likely origin of being *sent to Coventry*; looking back through the literary record, it's almost as if the phrase emerged out of nowhere sometime in the early 1700s. And with that absence of any kind of proof, plenty of alternative theories have emerged over the years purporting to fill in the etymological gap.

One explanation, for instance, claims that the phrase might allude to the poor treatment of the family of 'Peeping Tom', the legendary prankster who spied on Lady Godiva as she rode nude through the city of Coventry. Lady Godiva, however, lived during the eleventh century, and even the legend of her naked ride through the city did not emerge until the 1200s at least. If Peeping Tom were to blame for being *sent to Coventry*, we would presume to find more evidence of the expression between then and the mid 1700s.

Another theory claims that the phrase could in some way allude to Sir John Coventry. He was a seventeenth-century member of parliament who in 1670, after making a bawdy comment in the House of Commons about Charles II's love affair with a noted London actress, was set on by a number of the king's Royalist supporters and brutally mutilated.* The attack

---

* Coventry's nose was reportedly cut so deeply in the attack that the bone of his skull underneath was revealed. The *Oxford English Dictionary* ultimately lists an entry for a verb to *Coventry*, which it defines as 'to slit the nose of'.

caused an uproar, and led to the passing of the so-called Coventry Act, which stated:

> *That if any person shall, of malice aforethought, and by laying in wait, unlawfully cut or disable the tongue, put out an eye, slit the nose, cut off the nose or lip, or cut off or disable any limb, or member of any other person, with intent to maim or disfigure him, such person, his counsellors, aiders and abettors, shall be guilty of felony.*
> —*The Coventry Act* (22/23 Car. II, c.1)

But if this is the origin of being *sent to Coventry*, how did it come to mean 'to ostracise'? That's a question that casts a great deal of doubt on Sir John's involvement here.

And then there's this:

> *To send one to Coventry. A punishment inflicted by officers of the army on such of their brethren as are testy, or have been guilty of improper behaviour, not worthy the cognizance of a court martial. The person sent to Coventry is considered as absent; no one must speak to or answer any question he asks, except relative to duty, under penalty of being also sent to the same place. On a proper submission, the penitent is recalled, and welcomed by the mess, as just returned from a journey to Coventry.*
> —Francis Grose, *A Classical Dictionary of the Vulgar Tongue* (1785)

According to the lexicographer Francis Grose, who compiled this somewhat detailed description of being *sent to Coventry* in the late eighteenth century, the phrase appears to have had military connections. Could Grose's 'officers of the army' have known about the mistreatment of the Earl of Clarendon's Royalist troops, roughly a hundred and thirty years after the event? It seems unlikely. But, then again, perhaps we're looking too hard for an explanation here?

Perhaps Coventry was merely chosen at random, the place-holder name of a random city, of indiscriminate distance from the ostracised character in question; just as Grose points out, when the ostracism ends, it is almost as if the shunned person has merely 'returned from a journey to Coventry'. Perhaps being *sent to Coventry* could just as easily have been *sent to Glasgow*, *sent to Labrador* or *sent to Timbuktu*? Perhaps there's an absence of etymological proof here, because there was an absence of etymological reasoning in the first place?

Ironically, without any more etymological proof, it's impossible to say anything at all.

80

PORLOCK, UK

person from Porlock

Leaving Coventry behind us, we've just one more stop to make before we head back to London to complete our trip. We're travelling a hundred and twenty miles south-west as the crow flies, passing by Stratford, Gloucester, Bristol and the border with Wales and heading down into the far southwest corner of England.

The English southwest is one of the richest etymological seams we can mine. Its place names crop up in all manner of words and phrases, from *Cornish pasties* (an etymological relative of *pâté*, no less*) to the *Plymouth Brethren* (an Evangelical Christian movement that, despite its name, originated in Ireland†). If it's linguistic gold we're after, however, then we need

---

* As a word for a pie-like pastry, cooked without the need for a dish to enclose it, *pasty* derived from the French *paste*, which in turn comes from the French word for the meaty *pâté* (originally venison) that was baked inside them. Incredibly, in written English the word *pasty* was first recorded more than seven centuries ago in a document dated 1296. Even more incredibly, the earliest record of it comes from the surname of a gentleman from Warwickshire named 'Simon le Pasteymaker'.

† The name Plymouth Brethren, not chosen by the group itself, alludes to the fact that their first English meeting took place in Plymouth in 1831.

look no further than the enormous array of bizarre proverbs and curious sayings that the place names of the southwest of England has produced over the years.

When the tiny Cornish village of Mousehole was attacked by four Spanish galleys in 1595, for instance, no one from the nearby town of Penzance came to their neighbours' aid for fear of attracting the Spaniards' attention. As a result, *not a word of Penzance* became a proverbial expression for a total lack of help when help is most desperately needed.

To be like the mayor of Falmouth is to be in the wrong mood for the current state of affairs, or to celebrate something that in retrospect is none too celebratory. Lurking behind this bizarre expression, according to local folklore, is the fact that an unnamed mayor of Falmouth was once overheard celebrating that the town's gaol was finally being enlarged: a welcome development, certainly, but not a great sign that the town was heading in the right direction.

On the subject of criminals, *Lydford law*, named after the town of Lydford in Devon, is an ancient expression referring to summary justice – the execution of someone before a fair trial can be carried out. Reportedly, the cells in the Lydford jailhouse were so foul that those imprisoned in them died as a result of the awful conditions long before their trial could be heard.

And *'That's Exeter!' said the old woman when she saw Crediton* is an eighteenth-century Devonshire expression referring to that terrible moment when you think your work is done, but then find that even more needs doing. According to the story behind it, an unnamed old woman set off one day on the long walk from her home to Exeter market. On the way, she reached the top of a steep hill and finally saw on the horizon the impressive spires of Crediton's Church of the Holy Cross. Mistaking the church for Exeter Cathedral, the woman gleefully exclaimed, 'That's Exeter!', believing that her arduous journey was almost at an end. In fact, Crediton is a full eight miles from Exeter, and so her journey was still a long way from being complete.

Our journey, however, is almost over. We've no Crediton Hill to climb here – only a man to visit in nearby Porlock.

Some 40,000 miles ago, back in China, we heard how Samuel Taylor Coleridge, fuelled by opium and a copy of Samuel Purchas's *Pilgrimes*, imagined Kublai Khan's legendary capital of Xanadu. When he awoke, still fresh from his dream, Coleridge instantly put pen to paper and in the throes of inspiration composed some of the most famous lines in all English poetry. That, however, is only part of this story.

Coleridge's 'Kubla Khan' is only fifty-four lines long; its author apparently never finished it. When the poem was first published in 1816, Coleridge himself (writing in the third person) explained what happened:

> *On awakening he [Coleridge] appeared to himself to have a distinct recollection of the whole, and taking his pen, ink, and paper, instantly and eagerly wrote down the lines that are here preserved. At this moment he was unfortunately called out by a person on business from Porlock, and detained by him above an hour, and on his return to his room, found, to his no small surprise and mortification, that though he still retained some vague and dim recollection of the general purport of the vision, yet, with the exception of some eight or ten scattered lines and images, all the rest had passed away like the images on the surface of a stream into which a stone has been cast, but, alas! without the after restoration of the latter!*
> —Samuel Taylor Coleridge, *Christabel: Kubla Khan, a Vision; and the Pains of Sleep* (1816)

The identity of the 'person from Porlock' – a town on the Somerset coast – who disrupted Coleridge's creative flow is unknown (and indeed some later commentators have suggested that the visitor did not exist at all*). Nevertheless, the expression *person from Porlock*, or merely a *Porlock*, eventually fell into general use in English to describe someone who interrupts a writer's creative flow or, more loosely, someone who arrives at a wholly inopportune moment, or at the least convenient time turns up at your home.

---

* It's certainly possible that Coleridge merely invented his intrusive 'person from Porlock' as an excuse for not returning to, completing or tidying up the poem, or for not wanting to alter its off-the-cuff style. If this is the case, it would not be the only time Coleridge invented a distraction: chapter 13 of his *Biographia Literaria* (1817) opens as follows:

CHAPTER XIII
On the imagination, or esemplastic power
❀ ❀ ❀

Thus far had the work been transcribed for the press, when I received the following letter from a friend . . .

Coleridge goes on to write out the 'letter from a friend' word for word; he later revealed that he had written the letter himself.

EPILOGUE

London, UK

We have come full circle. The time has come to make the final journey across England from Porlock, on the Somerset coast, to London, where this all began some 70,000 miles, eighty destinations, sixty-five countries, and six continents ago.

On our way we've crossed deserts and oceans, dodged whirlpools and watched geysers, discovered a dozen new elements, twice improved children's nutrition, brewed up homemade liquor, dyed our hair (then ruined the furniture), viewed the unreachable, dodged the inevitable, and found out why Batman should have a Geordie accent – all without leaving home.

Our guide on this journey has been the dictionary, not the atlas, and it's hoped that this epic circumnavigation has illustrated how its stories and destinations are more varied, more bizarre and more surprising than you might ever have presumed.

But now, it's time to put your feet up. Don't be like the saddler of Bawtry* – pour yourself a drink.

* OK, one last story.

Bawtry is a small market town in South Yorkshire. Supposedly, a saddler (i.e. saddle-maker) from the town once fell foul of the law, and found himself sentenced to be hanged at the nearby gallows in the city of York. At the time, a tradition was in place that allowed anyone who had been condemned to die at the York gallows the chance of one final drink at a tavern on the outskirts of the city. The saddler, however, turned down the offer and so was taken straight from his jail cell to the gallows and hanged. Had he accepted the offer, however, a horseman who was en route with a last-minute reprieve from the local justice of the peace would have arrived in time to save his life. As it was, by turning down the drink, the saddler was somewhat unceremoniously killed.

Whether true or not, this macabre tale is at the root of the eighteenth-century expression *don't be like the saddler of Bawtry* – a casual nudge not to turn down the offer of a drink.

SELECT
BIBLIOGRAPHY

Brewer, E. Cobham. *Dictionary of Phrase and Fable*. Philadelphia, 1887.

Brewer, E. Cobham. *The Reader's Handbook of Famous Names in Fiction, Allusions, References, Proverbs, Plots, Stories and Poems*. Philadelphia, 1899.

Delahunty, Andrew, and Sheila Dignen. *Oxford Dictionary of Reference and Allusion* (3rd Ed.) Oxford, 2010.

Everett-Heath, John. *Oxford Concise Dictionary of World Place Names*. Oxford, 2005.

Green, Jonathon. *Words Apart: The Language of Prejudice*. London, 1996.

Green, Jonathon. *Chambers Slang Dictionary*. London, 2008.

Grose, Francis. *A Classical Dictionary of the Vulgar Tongue*. London, 1785.

Klein, Ernest. *A Comprehensive Etymological Dictionary of the English Language*. Amsterdam, 1971.

Liberman, Anatoly. *Analytic Dictionary of English Etymology*. Minneapolis, 2008.

Manser, Martin H., and David H. Pickering. *The Facts On File Dictionary of Classical and Biblical Allusions*. New York, 2003.

Nares, Robert. *A Glossary or Collection of Words, Phrases, Names, and Allusions [. . .] in the Works of English Authors, Particularly Shakespeare, and his Contemporaries*. London, 1859.

Partridge, Eric. *A Dictionary of Slang and Unconventional English* (8th Ed.) London, 1984.

Partridge, Eric. *The Routledge Dictionary of Historical Slang* (Revised 6th Ed.) London, 1973.

Partridge, Eric. *Name into Word: Proper Names That Have Become Common Property*. London, 1949.

Wright, Joseph. *The English Dialect Dictionary (Vols. 1–6)*. Oxford, 1896–1905.

ACKNOWLEDGEMENTS

With thanks as always to my agent, Andrew Lownie, and to Jennie Condell, Pippa Crane, Alison Menzies, and all at Elliott & Thompson for their advice, enthusiasm, guidance and – this time at least – unending patience. Thanks also to Chris Kirk, Louise Smith, Gav Howard and Anthony Edmundson, and a special mention, finally, to Ronnie Appleby.

Thanks all.